*Sharing the Gift*

# RESTORED

## EXPERIENCE LIFE WITH JESUS

---

### *Given to*

_____

*on this the_____ day of_____*

### *From*

_____

### *on the occasion of*

_____

# Praise for *Restored – Experience Life with Jesus*

"Countless people have found genuine freedom in Christ through the insights God has given Neil Anderson."

**– Kay Arthur**
*Executive Vice-President*, Precept Ministries Int'l

"Neil Anderson's Restored is filled with simple, clear Biblical principles that can lead anyone to spiritual freedom. The Holy Spirit ministered to me as I read. This is a wonderful book to share with others. I commend it to you!"

**– Dr. Paul Cedar**
*Chairman*, Mission America Coalition

"Restored is an indispensable tool for all who desire to live a life of freedom from unhealthy habits and painful pasts."

**– Hui Lin Chen**
*Director*, Campus Crusade Asia Limited Media

"I am so encouraged that the lives of many thousands of people have been profoundly changed through the ministry of Neil Anderson. What impresses me about him is his love of Christ, his deep knowledge of God's word, and his compassion for people."

**– Steve Douglass**
*President*, Campus Crusade For Christ

"After living more than 50 years as a Christian, and teaching more than 25 years as a professor of Bible and theology, I took about two hours to work carefully through Anderson's *'Steps to Freedom in Christ'* (The basis for *'Restored'*), God used that process to impart to me a wonderfully refreshing sense of freedom, peace, joy and fellowship with Himself.[1]

**– Dr. Wayne Grudem**
Professor of Theology, Phoenix Seminary

"Neil Anderson represents Jesus as the champion of the broken. Restored is a full-dimensioned message of redeeming and regenerating grace that provides a future unfolding full restoration and recovery."

**– Jack W. Hayford**
*President*, International Foursquare Churches
*Chancellor*, The King's College and Seminary

1. Anderson, Neil, Praying By The Power of the Holy Spirit, Regal Books, Ventura, California, 2003.

# RESTORED
## EXPERIENCE LIFE WITH JESUS

# Dr. Neil T. Anderson

e3 Resources
Franklin, Tennessee, U.S.A.

**Restored**
**Experience Life with Jesus**
Published and Distributed by e3 Resources,
317 Main Street Suite 207
Franklin, TN 37064

w w w . e 3 r e s o u r c e s . o r g

e3 Resources is a non-profit ministry based in Franklin, TN. Our mission is to develop innovative tools for the Body of Christ to use in effectively implementing their prayer, evangelism, and discipleship strategies for the glory of God. e3 Resources is a division of e3 Partners, based in Dallas, TX.

*For other e3 Resources products please call your Christian supplier or contact us at*: **888-354-9411** or **www.e3resources.org**.

Unless otherwise marked, all Scripture references taken from
the NEW AMERICAN STANDARD BIBLE®, Copyright © 1960, 1962,
1963, 1968, 1671, 1672, 1673, 1975, 1977 by The Lockman Foundation.
Used by permission.

Verses marked KJV are taken from the King James Version of the Bible.

Verses marked NKJV are taken from the New King James Version,
Copyright ©1979, 1980, 1982 by Thomas Nelson, Inc., Publishers.
Used by permission.

Library of Congress Cataloging-in-Publication Data
Anderson, Neil T. 1942-
Restored : experience life with Jesus/ Neil T. Anderson.
p. cm.
ISBN-10: 1-933383-39-9 (trade paperback)
ISBN-13: 978-1-933383-39-2 (trade paperback)
1. Christian Living. 2. Discipleship. 3. New Believer. 4. Christian Growth.
I. Title.
2006940084

*Printed in the United States of America*

# Contents

*I dedicate this book to the memory of*

## Dr. Stephen King

*This humble man was a missionary doctor,
psychiatrist, devoted family man, and
board member of Freedom in Christ Ministries.
He believed in the message of this book
and the restoring work of the
Wonderful Counselor and Great Physician.
Stephen is now in the presence of God,
along with thousands of people
he led to the Lord, doctored, and counseled.
His devoted wife, Judy, and the rest of us
who have been touched by Stephen's life
will join him in eternity.
Thank you, Dr. Stephen King,
for your exemplary life of Christian service.*

# Introduction

"If Christ had been too proud to die, he could not have helped us whose basic sin is pride. So Paul and others argue that by giving Himself up without pride, Christ makes up for Adam's sin of arrogance. If all this is true it comprises certainly the most momentous fact of human existence. Christ the free therapist for humanity, bringing salvation as a gift of grace-that indeed is a daring postulate."

**– Rollo May**

---

*"The time is fulfilled, and the kingdom of God is at hand; repent and believe in the Gospel."*[1]

**– Jesus**

---

You have just made the greatest decision of your life, or maybe you are still considering what becoming a Christian really means. The moment you decide to trust in the saving work of the Lord Jesus Christ, you become a new creation in Him,[2] and you will be spiritually transferred from the kingdom of darkness to the Kingdom of God,[3] and enter into eternal life. Although you may not immediately feel like any great change has taken place, your life and destiny have changed forever.

Countless millions of people before you have made the same decision and have become a part of God's unfolding plan to restore a fallen humanity. God has known you and loved you before you were even born. He has prepared a place for you in His kingdom, and He has a plan just for you.[4] If you receive Him as your Lord and Savior, you will discover the eternal purpose and meaning of life.

Salvation is so much more than knowing why we are here. If you are willing to repent and believe the Gospel you will discover that Jesus is the Wonderful Counselor and the Great Physician. He came to set captives free and bind up the broken hearted. Jesus is the "free therapist for humanity", and the purpose of this book is to establish you alive and free in Christ through genuine repentance and faith in God. Jesus loves you and wants you to fulfill your destiny as a liberated child of God.

# CHAPTER ONE
## REDEMPTION HISTORY

We have learned from history that most people haven't learned much from history. Those who don't learn are doomed to repeat the same failures over and over again. Those who have learned the truth from their forefathers know that history is His-story of unfolding grace and love for all humanity. In order to understand what His plan is for you, we need to start at the beginning of human history.

## THE CREATION

"In the beginning God created the heavens and the earth,"[5] are the first words in the Bible. God is a Spirit and is infinite, eternal, and unchangeable in His wisdom, power and holiness. He existed when the physical world was just an idea. There was a beginning in time when He created all physical matter and all living creatures. Then

God created Adam in His image, and together with Eve they were to rule over the birds of the sky, the beasts of the field, and the fish of the sea.[6] They had dominion over the rest of creation and were to be fruitful in order to multiply and fill the earth. They were physically alive, which means their souls were in union with their bodies. They were spiritually alive; therefore their souls were in union with God. Because they were created in the image of God, they could think, feel, and make choices, unlike all the other creatures that are physically alive, which function by divine instinct.

Adam and Eve were safe, secure, and significant. They had a sense of belonging to God and to each other. They were naked and unashamed because they had nothing to hide and therefore no need to cover up. Adam and Eve were welcomed to eat from the Tree of Life and live forever by remaining in union with God.

Prior to the creation of humanity, a magnificent angel named Lucifer rebelled against the Creator God and fell from heaven, taking a third of the angels with him. Lucifer means light bearer, but he no longer reflected the glory of God. He became Satan, or the devil, and ruled over his brood of fallen angels, known in the Bible as demons. Jealous for the significant position Adam and Eve were given, Satan tempted Eve to eat the forbidden fruit. She in turn persuaded Adam to do so, and together they sinned by rebelling against God.

# THE FALL

The consequences were immediate. Adam and Eve died spiritually. Sin had separated them from God. Their souls were no longer in union with their Heavenly Father. They remained physically alive, but physical death would be a consequence of their sin as well.

Adam and Eve were left to make a name for themselves and to find their purpose and meaning in life independent of their Heavenly Father. They had to rely on their own strength and resources because the life of God was no longer within them. They were like cars without gas and struggled to find purpose and meaning in life in their natural state, which is still true to this day for those who don't have a relationship with God.

Every car has a battery that provides a spark of life, so the natural person tries to find their purpose in the beauty of the car, or the comfort of the seats, or the sound of the stereo, or the lights, or the noise of the horn, but that is not what the car was created for. The purpose of automobiles is to supply transportation. Without gas they may look, sound, smell, and feel good, but they cannot fulfill their purpose for which they were created, and neither can we unless we have the life of Christ within us.

As a consequence of the fall, every natural descendent of Adam and Eve is born physically alive, but spiritually dead.[7] In addition, the whole world was affected by their rebellion, and all creation is groaning and looking forward to a day of redemption.[8] That day is coming because God immediately cursed the devil and promised that a descendent of Eve would bring forth a Savior that would crush the head of Satan.[9]

God's plan was to first show all humanity their need for a Savior. He revealed our need by instituting a sacrificial system to show us that somebody had to pay the penalty for our sins, and through Moses God gave us a moral law to govern our behavior. However, no animal sacrifice could give us spiritual life, and nobody could live according to the law. So He sent prophets encouraging His people to live righteously according to the laws of God. These prophets also revealed God's word to us and recorded the history of God's redemptive plan. There are 39 books in the Old Testament that record the history of creation and the fall of Adam and Eve. They reveal humanity's futile attempts to find purpose and meaning in life and live independently of God.

God called Abraham out of the Land of Ur, which is the land of present day Iraq, and into the promised land of Israel. With Abraham, God made an unconditional covenant, promising that through him and his descendents all the nations of the earth would be blessed. The Messiah would come from one of His descendents. Through the prophet Moses, God made a conditional covenant of law, promising to bless those who kept it, but none could. For centuries God's chosen people tried unsuccessfully to live under the law, which proved to be a taskmaster that was intended by God to lead us to Christ,[10] the promised Messiah.

# THE GOSPEL

When it looked liked there was no hope for humanity, and when the time was just right, God sent Jesus His Son. Jesus was supernaturally born of the Virgin Mary and, like Adam, was born both physically and spiritually alive. Jesus is the pre-existent Word of God who became flesh and dwelt amongst us. Jesus is co-equal with the Father and the Holy Spirit, and together they make up the One true God. While on this earth Jesus remained fully God, but He was also fully human. No person can become God, but God can and did manifest Himself in human form. Jesus came for three primary reasons.

> All temptation is an attempt to get us to live our lives independently of God.

First, He came to give us an example to follow in His steps. Jesus showed us how a spiritually alive person could live a righteous life. He did so by demonstrating a life totally dependent upon His Heavenly Father.[11] All temptation is an attempt to get us to live our lives independently of God. Jesus was tempted in all ways, but unlike Adam, He never sinned. His sinless perfection was what made Jesus the only possible sacrifice for our sins. No other animal or human sacrifice could accomplish that.

Sin had separated all humanity from God, and the wages of sin is death.[12] So Jesus went to the cross to die for our sins in order that we may be forgiven. According to the Old Testament Law, there is no forgiveness without the shedding of blood.[13] In dying and shedding His blood, Jesus removed the enmity that existed between God and all humanity. "He [God the Father] made Him [Jesus] who knew no sin to be sin on our behalf, so that we might become the righteousness of God."[14] However, knowing that our sins are forgiven is not enough.

Second, Jesus came not only to die on the cross for our sins, but also to be resurrected in order that we may have new eternal, i.e. spiritual, life in Christ. That means our souls are again in union with God. What Adam and Eve lost in the fall was life, and what Jesus came to give us was life.[15] "Jesus is the bread of life."[16] He is "the way, the truth and the life."[17] He is the only path back to God. "And there is salvation in no one else; for there is no other name under heaven that has been given among men by which we must be saved.[18] "Jesus is the truth and if you know the truth, the truth will set you free."[19] Jesus said, "I am the resurrection and the life; he who believes in Me will live [spiritually] even if he dies [physically], and everyone who lives and believes in Me will never die [spiritually]. [20]

## SAVED BY THE GRACE OF GOD THROUGH FAITH

The only way we can enter into this new life is by putting our faith and trust totally in God and relying on the work of Christ alone to save us. "For by grace you have been saved through faith; and that not of yourselves, it is the gift of God; not as a result of works, so that no one may boast."[21] If you have never received this free gift from God, why don't you do so right now? God knows your heart, and you can respond to Him by praying:

> *Dear Heavenly Father, thank You for sending Jesus to die on the cross for my sins. I acknowledge that I have sinned and that I cannot save myself. I believe that Jesus came to give me eternal and spiritual life, and by faith I now choose to receive You into my life as my Lord and my Savior. By the power of Your indwelling presence, enable me to be the person You created me to be. I pray that You would grant me repentance leading to a knowledge of the truth, so that I can experience my new identity and freedom in Christ and be transformed by the renewing of my mind. In Jesus' precious name I pray. Amen.*

The Apostle John wrote, "As many as received Him, to them He gave the right to become children of God, to those who believe in His name."[22] "See how great a love the Father has bestowed on us, that we would be called children of God; and such we are."[23] Jesus instructed His disciples to address our prayers to, "Our Father who is in heaven,"[24] which also means that we are His children. Knowing who you are as a child of God is critical for your growth in Christ and in becoming the person God intends you to be. No person can consistently behave in a way that is inconsistent with what they believe about themselves. That is why the Holy Spirit bears witness with our spirit that we are children of God.[25]  Our heavenly Father wants us to know that we are His children.

Yet Jesus came not only came to die for our sins and give us new life in Him, but also to supply all our needs according to His riches in glory in Christ Jesus.[26]  He gave us life, and this life gives us our true identity as children of God. He meets our needs of acceptance, security, and significance as follows:

## IN CHRIST

### *I am accepted*:

| | |
|---|---|
| John 1:12 | I am God's child. |
| John 15:15 | I am Jesus' chosen friend. |
| Romans 5:1 | I have been made holy and accepted by God (justified). |
| 1 Corinthians 6:17 | I am united with the Lord and one with Him in spirit. |
| 1 Corinthians6:20 | I have been bought with a price-- I belong to God. |
| 1 Corinthians 12:27 | I am a member of Christ's body, part of His family. |
| Ephesians 1:1 | I am a saint, a holy one. |
| Ephesians 1:5 | I have been adopted as God's child. |
| Ephesians 2:18 | I have direct access to God through the Holy Spirit. |
| Colossians 1:14 | I have been bought back (redeemed) and forgiven of all my sins. |
| Colossians 2:10 | I am complete in Christ. |

## *I am secure:*

| | |
|---|---|
| Romans 8:1, 2 | I am free forever from punishment (condemnation). |
| Romans 8:28 | I am assured that all things work together for my good. |
| Romans 8:31F | I am free from any condemning charges against me. |
| Romans 8:35F | I cannot be separated from the love of God. |
| 2 Corinthians 1:21 | I have been established, anointed, and sealed by God. |
| Colossians 3:3 | I am hidden with Christ in God. |
| Philippians 1:6 | I am sure the good work God has started in me will be finished. |
| Philippians 3:20 | I am a citizen of heaven. |
| 2 Timothy 1:7 | I have not been given a spirit of fear, but of power, love, and a sound mind. |
| Hebrews 4:16 | I can find grace and mercy in time of need. |
| 1 John 5:18 | I am born of God and the evil one cannot touch me. |

## *I am significant:*

| | |
|---|---|
| Matthew 5:13 | I am salt and light for everyone around me. |
| John 15:1-5 | I am a part of the true vine, joined to Christ and able to produce much fruit. |
| John 15:16 | I have been handpicked by Jesus to bear fruit. |
| Acts 1:8 | I am a personal witness of Christ's. |
| 1 Corinthians 3:16 | I am God's temple where the Holy Spirit lives. |

| | |
|---|---|
| 2 Corinthians 5:17F | I am at peace with God, and He has given me the work of making peace between Himself and other people. I am a minister of reconciliation. |
| 2 Corinthians 6:1 | I am God's co-worker. |
| Ephesians 2:6 | I am seated with Christ in the heavenly places. |
| Ephesians 2:10 | I am God's workmanship. |
| Ephesians 3:12 | I may approach God with freedom and confidence. |
| Philippians 4:13 | I can do all things through Christ who strengthens me. |

All these statements are true because of our union with God. This new life in Christ, which is our union with God, is most often referred to in the Bible as being "in Christ" or "in Him." For every verse in the Bible that talks about Christ being in God's children, there are ten verses that talk about God's children being "in Christ." For instance, the six chapters of the book of Ephesians contain forty references to being "in Christ." In total, there are 27 books in the New Testament. The first four are historical and are called the gospels, which describe the birth, life, death, burial, and resurrection of Christ. The fifth book of Acts is an historical book depicting the life of the early church and the work of the Apostles, who also wrote the rest of the New Testament under the inspiration of the Holy Spirit. These Epistles provide instruction for the church, which is the living body of Christ. The entire Bible was written over a period of

1400 years by forty different authors who all wrote under the inspiration of God. The Bible is therefore the authoritative Word for life and practice of all God's people.

After Jesus was resurrected, He appeared to His disciples and hundreds of others who were still alive when the New Testament was being written.[27] He was with them for around fifty days, and then went home to Heaven. He now sits at the right hand of God the Father, which is the spiritual throne and the seat of authority for the universe. After Jesus was glorified in Heaven, the Holy Spirit was sent to all those who believe in the finished work of Jesus. The pouring out of the Holy Spirit came at the Jewish feast of Pentecost, which marks the beginning of the Church. The Holy Spirit is the Spirit of Truth[28] and dwells in every believer the moment they are born again spiritually. The Holy Spirit will lead you into all truth, and that truth will set you free.

## The Defeat of Satan

There is a third reason that Jesus came. He came to undo the works of Satan.[29] Because Adam and Eve sinned, they forfeited their dominion over this earth, and Satan became the rebel holder of authority. Jesus referred to him as the ruler of this world[30] but promised that he would be cast out.[31] The Apostle John wrote that the whole world lies in the power of the evil one[32] because he deceives the whole world.[33] But Jesus disarmed Satan[34] when He defeated sin and death at the cross by His own death and resurrection.

Knowing that Satan and his demons are defeated is just as much a part of the gospel as the fact that your sins are forgiven and that you have new life in Christ. People all over the world are terrorized by Satan and his demons. Satan is the father of lies,[35] and people are in bondage to those lies. The false religions of this world try to appease him and manipulate the spiritual world through their Satanic worship and the incantations of their shamans. Satan wants to be feared because he wants to be worshiped above God. But only God is worthy of worship because He alone is omnipotent (all powerful), omnipresent (everywhere present), and omniscient (all knowing), and every true believer is seated with Christ in the heavenlies,[36] which is the spiritual realm.

> Power
> is the ability
> to rule,
> and authority
> is the right
> to rule.
> In Christ
> we have both.

All authority has been given to Jesus in heaven and upon this earth,[37] and on that basis we are commissioned to go into this world and make disciples[38] and teach them to believe all that He said. That means that Satan has no authority over any of God's children. Because of our union with God, we have the authority and the power to do God's will. Power is the ability to rule, and authority is the right to rule. In Christ we have both. That is why the Apostle Paul wrote, "Finally, be strong in the Lord and in the strength of His might."[39] As children of God, we live by faith in God, in His strength and by His authority. If we try to do His will in our own strength and by our own authority, we will fail miserably. We have no spiritual authority to do our own will independent of our Heavenly Father, but we have the authority to do God's will, and this authority is over the kingdom of darkness, which includes Satan and all his demons.

## A CALL TO REPENTANCE

Paul's instruction to the church included more than belief in God. He also taught "that they should repent and turn to God, performing deeds appropriate to repentance."[40] The Apostle Peter said to the early church, "Repent, and each of you be baptized in the name of Jesus Christ for the forgiveness of your sins; and you will receive the gift of the Holy Spirit. For the promise is for you and your children and for all who are far off, as many as the Lord our God will call to Himself.[41] Circumcision was a sign of the Old Testament Covenant of Law, and baptism is a sign of the New Testament Covenant of Grace, which identifies the believer with the life, death, burial, and resurrection of Christ.

We are saved by the grace of God through faith in the finished work of Christ, but if we want to experience our new life and freedom in Christ and grow by the grace of God, we must repent of our sins. The rest of this book will lead you through a repentance process. If you are completely honest with God during the process, you will sense His presence in your life when you are finished: "And the peace of God which surpasses all comprehension, will guard your hearts and your minds in Christ Jesus.[42]

You are also admonished to seek baptism in your local church and publicly declare your faith in Jesus. "If you confess with your mouth Jesus as Lord, and believe in your heart that God raised Him from the dead, you will be saved; for with the heart a person believes, resulting in righteousness, and with the mouth he confesses, resulting in salvation."[43]

# CHAPTER TWO
## OVERCOMING FALSE GUIDANCE

If you really want to experience your freedom in Christ, the first step is to renounce previous or current involvement with any activity or group that denies Jesus Christ, offers guidance through sources contrary to the Word of God, or requires secret ceremonies or covenants. The Bible teaches that "he who conceals his sins does not prosper, but whoever confesses and renounces them finds mercy."[44] *Renounce* means to *forsake* or *say no to* something or someone. Renounce is the first step toward repentance, which means to turn away from something and towards something else. *Repentance* literally means *a change of mind*, but it is much more comprehensive in its application.

When the Pharisees and the Sadducees came to be baptized by John, "He said to them, 'You brood of vipers, who warned you to flee from the wrath to come? Therefore bring forth fruit in keeping with repentance."[45] Jesus knew their repentance was incomplete. They wanted the blessing of God but didn't want to give up their traditions, practices, and religious positions.

## THE NEED TO RENOUNCE

The public declaration: "I renounce you Satan and all your works and all your ways" has historically been a part of the Church's profession of faith since its earliest days. To this day members of most liturgical churches are encouraged to make that public profession at salvation or confirmation. In the Early Church, believers would literally face west and make that declaration. Then they would face east and declare their belief in God. The statement is only generic, however. Every work of Satan and every way of Satan had to be renounced in order for repentance to be complete.

If we declare something as true, then it is just as important to declare the counterfeit as false.

To be free from the past, it is necessary to specifically renounce every false religion, false teacher, false practice, and every means of false guidance you have participated in. Many people come to Christ and make a profession of faith, but continue in their old ways of seeking guidance and in participation in false religious practices. That is not complete repentance. If we declare something as true, then it is just as important to declare the counterfeit as false. You cannot believe the truth and believe a lie at the same time and experience your freedom in Christ.

The Cross dealt with the forgiveness of our sins. The Resurrection provided us with new life in Christ, and the Ascension of Christ to the right hand of the Father assured us of the authority and power to live a victorious life in Christ. But the moment we are born again, our minds are not totally renewed. That is why Paul said, "Do not be conformed to this world, but be transformed by the renewing of your mind, that you may prove what the will of God is, that which is good and acceptable and perfect."[46] The Cross, the Resurrection, and the Ascension make all that possible. Now we can repent and renew our minds. We can renounce the lies, the false guidance, and the false teachers. And we can choose the truth as led by the Holy Spirit.

## DEMONIC FORCES AT WORK

The Apostle Paul warned us what we can expect in this world: "But the Spirit explicitly says that in later times some will fall away from the faith, paying attention to deceitful spirits and doctrines of demons."[47] Concerning the last days, Jesus said, "For false Christs and false prophets will arise and will show great signs and wonders, so as to mislead, if possible, even the elect."[48] These deceptive belief systems and false teachings are counterfeits. They may appear to mimic the truth, but they are in fact satanically inspired lies. They are taught by false teachers who often represent themselves as followers of Christ.[49]

When assessing counterfeits of Christianity, no criterion is more important than the doctrine of Jesus Christ. If any person or group will not or cannot say that Jesus Christ is the Son of God, the King of kings, and the great I AM, then they should be considered suspect.[50] Many people under the influence of Satan can say that Jesus is Lord, but when asked to say Jesus is their Lord, they simply repeat, "Jesus is Lord." The Devil knows that Jesus is the Lord of the universe, but will not profess Jesus as his Lord, nor will his followers.

> Genuine repentance is the means by which we experience our freedom, as we renounce the lies and choose the truth.

A second identifiable trait of false religions and the occult is an offer of salvation or enlightenment through something other than faith in the finished work of Christ. Satan blinds the minds of people to the gospel of Jesus Christ.[51] New Age proponents teach that we are not separated from God by our sin and therefore have no need to repent. They say we are God and only need to be enlightened. What a lie!

Third, psychics, gurus, shamans, and false prophets offer a special quality of life, esoteric knowledge, or special power that is available by connecting with cosmic energy sources, secret rituals, ceremonies, or covenants. Occult means hidden, concealed or secret, which is in total contrast to the nature of God, who does everything in the light. What is really hidden from view, however, is Satan, the puppet master. His goal is to keep humanity in bondage by drawing us away from the truth that would set us free. Genuine repentance is the means by which we experience our freedom, as we renounce the lies and choose the truth.

## TAKING A VERBAL STAND

The believer has a responsibility to submit to God and resist the devil.[52] In doing so they are recognizing God's authority over their lives and His authority over the demonic realm.[53] They are taking their rightful position at Christ's right hand and standing against the devil, using the sword of the Spirit, which is the Word of God. They are exercising dependence upon God and the authority they have in Christ.

The Bible relates the story of unregenerate men who tried to exert authority over the demonic realm by using rituals and incantations. Such futility will bring disastrous results. The seven sons of Sceva were unbelievers trying to cast out demons in Jesus' name without an authentic relationship with Him.[54] They were stripped of their clothes, beaten up, and kicked out. Their efforts were similar to occultic practices that try to manipulate the spirit world to do their will, but not God's will.

The biblical example of breaking counterfeit religious ties with the past is found in Acts 19:18-20. Many of the new Christians in Ephesus had been deeply involved in false religions and the occult through worship at the Temple of Artemis. Luke writes in verse 18, "Many also of those who had believed kept coming, confessing and disclosing their practices." The open disclosure of occult practices was followed by the positive action of ridding themselves of anything associated with that darkness. "And many of those who practiced magic brought their books together and began burning them in the sight of all."

# BRINGING EVERYTHING INTO THE LIGHT

God knows what needs to be brought into the light. You may not be totally aware of some previous religious experiences that have given a foothold to the enemy. That is why you are encouraged to pray and ask God to bring to your mind all previous involvement with cult or occult practices, false religions, and false teachers, whether done knowingly or unknowingly. Two important objectives will be accomplished in this first step. First, mental strongholds that came from false belief systems will be exposed and broken by agreeing with God through verbal renunciation. Second, you will learn how to handle lies and strongholds that surface later. This step will enable you to recognize the counterfeits, and know how to deal with them in the future.

Begin these Steps to Freedom in Christ with the following prayer and declaration.

## PRAYER

*Dear heavenly Father, You are present in this room and in my life. You alone are all-knowing, all-powerful and everywhere present, and I worship You alone. I declare my dependency upon You, for apart from You I can do nothing. I choose to believe Your Word, which teaches that all authority in heaven and earth belongs to the resurrected Christ, and being alive in Christ I have the authority to resist the devil as I submit to You. I ask that You fill me with Your Holy Spirit and guide me into all truth. I ask for Your complete protection and guidance as I seek to know You and do Your will. In the wonderful name of Jesus I pray. Amen.*

## DECLARATION

*In the name and authority of the Lord Jesus Christ, I command Satan and all evil spirits to release their hold on me in order that I can be free to know and choose to do the will of God.*

*As a child of God who is seated with Christ in the heavenly places, I declare that every enemy of the Lord Jesus Christ in my presence be bound. Satan and all his demons cannot inflict any pain or in any way prevent God's will from being done in my life today, because I belong to the Lord Jesus Christ.*

## BEGINNING STEP ONE

If you are processing all the Steps at once (recommended), then you need only do it once. However, if you are processing these Steps to Freedom one step or chapter at a time, then begin each chapter (Step) with the above prayer and declaration. As you begin this repentance process, you are taking back any ground gained by the enemy in your life, issue by issue, and step-by-step. To help you understand the spiritual significance of what you are doing, consider the following illustration:

Suppose there is a 40-year-old man who has never done much right in his life. At a church service, for the first time in his life, he hears about Jesus. His heart responds to the gospel, and he prays, "Lord, I confess that I have sinned. Thank You for dying on the cross for my sins. I choose to believe that You were raised from the dead in order that I may have eternal life. I now receive You into my life as my Lord and Savior."

If you and I were in the room when that man prayed, we may not have seen anything happen visibly. But in the spiritual realm, his sins were forgiven, he passed from death to life and from eternity in hell to eternity in heaven. All of this happened because he wanted to be right with God. God hears and answers prayer, and neither Satan nor his demons, nor any other person could block what God wanted to do in that man's life.

We're going to go through a series of prayers now. Many of them are short, simple prayers like the one that man prayed. As you are honest and sincere before God, every prayer you pray is going to be like the prayer of that man. Bonds the enemy has on your life will be broken because of your authority as God's child.

To successfully process this first step and those that follow, find a quiet place where you can pray each prayer out loud and verbally process each step. This action is important because there is no indication in the Bible that Satan can read your mind. God knows your innermost thoughts, but Satan is not God, and we should never ascribe the divine attributes of God unto him.

If you experience some mental interference, just ignore it and continue on. Thoughts such as This isn't going to work or I don't believe this, or blasphemous, condemning, and accusing thoughts have no power over you unless you believe them. They are just thoughts, but if you pay attention to them, you may be paying attention to a deceiving spirit and that will stop the process. Such thoughts will be gone after you have fully repented and finished the last step. The mind is the control center, and if you don't lose control of your mind, you will not lose control during the process.

Some people experience physical symptoms like nausea or headaches. Just ignore them and go on with the steps. They too will disappear at the end. If you cannot stay mentally focused, call your pastor and ask him to help you through the process. The book *Discipleship Counseling* (Regal Books, 2003) explains the process.

Most people going through these Steps don't encounter much opposition. The enemy isn't the issue anyway. Our relationship with God is the real issue. These Steps remove barriers to our intimacy with our heavenly Father. Going through these Steps is the process of submitting to God and resisting the devil according to James 4:7. If there is no devil or demons to resist it doesn't make any difference, because these seven steps are issues affecting our relationship with God.

## PRAYING FOR THE RIGHT GUIDANCE

The first step toward experiencing your freedom in Christ is to renounce (verbally reject) all involvement (past or present) with occult, cult, or false religious teachings or practices. Participation in any group that denies that Jesus Christ is Lord and/or elevates any teaching or book to the level of or a level above the Bible must be renounced. In addition, groups that require dark, secret initiations, ceremonies, vows, pacts, or covenants need to be renounced. God does not take lightly false guidance. "As for the person who turns to mediums and to spiritists... I will also set My face against that person and will cut him off from among my people" (Leviticus 20:6). Since you don't want the Lord to cut you off, ask Him to guide you as follows:

> *Dear Heavenly Father, please bring to my mind anything and everything that I have done knowingly or unknowingly that involves occult, cult, or false religious teachings or practices. I want to experience Your freedom by renouncing any and all false guidance. In Jesus' name I pray.* **Amen.**

The Lord may bring events to your mind that you had forgotten, even experiences you participated in as a game or thought was a joke. You might even have been passively or curiously watching others participate in counterfeit religious practices. The purpose is to renounce all counterfeit spiritual experiences and their beliefs.

To help bring these things to your mind, prayerfully consider the following Non-Christian Spiritual Checklist. Then pray the prayer following the checklist to renounce each activity or group the Lord brings to mind. He may also reveal to you ones that are not on the list. Be especially aware of your need to renounce non-Christian folk religious practices if you have grown up in another culture. It is important that you prayerfully renounce them out loud.

## Non-Christian Spiritual Checklist
Check all those that you have participated in:

- ❏ Out of Body Experience
- ❏ Ouija Board
- ❏ Bloody Mary
- ❏ Occult Games
- ❏ Magic Eight Ball
- ❏ Spells or Curses
- ❏ Mental Telepathy/Control
- ❏ Automatic Writing
- ❏ Trance
- ❏ Spirit Guides
- ❏ Fortune Telling/Divination
- ❏ Tarot Cards
- ❏ Levitation
- ❏ Witchcraft/Wicca/Sorcery
- ❏ Satanism
- ❏ Palm Reading
- ❏ Astrology/Horoscopes
- ❏ Hypnosis
- ❏ Astral Projection
- ❏ Seances/Mediums/Channelers

- ❑ Black or White Magic
- ❑ Blood Pacts
- ❑ Fetishism/Crystals/Charms
- ❑ Sexual Spirits
- ❑ Martial Arts (Mysticism)
- ❑ Jehovah's Witness
- ❑ New Age (Teachings, Medicine)
- ❑ Masons
- ❑ Christian Science/Mind Science
- ❑ Unification Church (Moonies)
- ❑ The Forum
- ❑ Church of Scientology
- ❑ Unitarianism/Universalism
- ❑ Yoga (Religion, not the Exercise)
- ❑ Hare Krishna
- ❑ Baha'ism
- ❑ Native American Spirit Worship
- ❑ Islam
- ❑ Hinduism
- ❑ Buddhism (including Zen)
- ❑ Black Muslim
- ❑ Rosicrucianism
- ❑ False gods:
  money, sex, power, pleasure, certain people
- ❑ Other:
  non-Christian religions, cults, movies, music
  books, video games, comics, fantasy games that
  glorify Satan that precipitated nightmares or
  mental battles, and all other questionable
  spiritual experiences including spiritual
  visitations and nightmares

## *Additional questions to help you become aware of counterfeit religious experiences:*

1. Do you now have, or have you ever had, an imaginary friend, spirit guide, or "angel" offering you guidance or companionship? If it has a name, renounce it by name.

2. Have you ever heard voices in your head or had repeating, nagging thoughts such as "I'm dumb," "I'm ugly," "Nobody loves me," "I can't do anything right"—as if there were a conversation going on inside your head? You should renounce paying attention to deceiving spirits.

3. Have you ever been hypnotized, attended a New Age seminar, or consulted a medium or spiritist? You should renounce each experience.

4. Have you ever made a secret vow or pact or inner vow? (i.e., "I will never . . .") You should renounce such vows and pacts.

5. Have you ever been involved in a satanic ritual or attended a concert in which Satan was the focus? You should renounce such experiences.

Once you have completed your checklist and the questions, confess and renounce every false religious practice, belief, ceremony, vow or pact that you were involved in by praying the following prayer aloud:

*Lord Jesus,* I confess that I have participated in (specifically name every belief and involvement with all that you have checked on the spiritual checklist), *and I renounce them all as counterfeits. I pray that You will fill me with Your Holy Spirit that I may be guided by You. Thank You that in Christ I am forgiven.* **Amen.**

If you have been involved in a false religion, you need to renounce specific beliefs and practices that you have participated in. For instance, if you came out of the Mormon religion, you may need to renounce the secret initiation you had and the ceremonies in baptisms and marriages for the dead in which you participated. If you are unsure whether a previous practice was false or not, but God is bringing it to your remembrance, you can be nearly certain it is something to renounce.

One area that sometimes needs explanation is sexual spirits. Demons may manifest themselves in vivid sexual dreams or fantasies or by a demonic presence in the room that aroused you sexually. Extreme cases will be vile in nature. If you stood against it at the time, there is nothing to renounce. It is no sin to be under attack. If you participated with the sexual spirits, then you need to renounce any involvement and every sexual use of your body as an instrument of unrighteousness.

The "Non-Christian Spiritual Checklist," is not exhaustive, so when you have finished checking off the items, ask the Lord if there is anything else you have participated in that you should renounce. Let the Holy Spirit bring those items to your mind. Any number of things might surface: books, photos, movies, music, or other materials, religious customs or traditions, praying to idols or angels by name, beliefs such as atheism, agnosticism, hedonism, or pharisaic control groups.

**You must assume responsibility for your own thoughts.**

Some believe they don't have a choice, but they do, and so do you. Consider the following illustration:

> If I were to come to your house tonight and knock on your door, you would first come to the door to see who is there, and then you would have a choice to make. You could open the door to allow me to come in, or you could close the door to deny me access. In the same way, when the enemy tries to invade your mind with lies and accusations, you have a choice to make. You can choose to allow those thoughts to come in, or you can deny them access. To "open the door" to enemy lies, you simply remain passive. You let him set the agenda for your thoughts. To "close the door," you take your thoughts captive to the obedience of Christ. You can choose to believe the truth or you can choose to believe a lie. You can choose to think bad thoughts, or you can choose to think upon that which is lovely, pure, and right. It is your choice.

You must assume responsibility for your own thoughts. You may not realize how passive you have been about entertaining deceptive thoughts. Others have never even considered the possibility of not obeying what they are paying attention to. In some difficult cases, a person will continue to be bombarded with thoughts that sound like voices in the head. If this happens, consider the following illustration:

> Suppose we're trying to carry on a conversation in a room where there are speakers playing loud music or there is a talk show blaring on the television set. If we wanted to continue our conversation, we would have to simply ignore the speakers. In the same way, you can choose to ignore those voices or thoughts. You can choose to believe, "I'm a child of God, and I will continue to work through the issues and find my freedom in Christ."

When you exercise your authority in Christ that way, the symptoms usually subside, but it probably won't be completely over until the last Step. Remember, they are just distracting noises and thoughts.

To make this Step complete, you should discard any books, photos, materials, artifacts, music, or any other items or gifts you own that may be tied to anything on the list. These may be symbols of allegiance to other gods, and if so, they are counterproductive to walking in the Kingdom of light. Follow the example found in Acts 19:19, where believers got rid of anything associated with darkness. Recognizing that Satan could continue to use the tools of their former religious practices, they publicly destroyed about 50,000 days' wages worth of books, which is a mind-boggling sum. These New Testament believers would make any sacrifice to be rid of Satan's influence in their lives and prevent further influence in their families.

## CHOOSE THE TRUTH

While going through the Steps, you may have discerned specific events that have had a dramatic effect on your life, or specific lies you have believed. Hopefully you directly renounced them. For example, a woman had nagging fears and anxieties about her experiences with her aunt who was heavily involved in witchcraft. She was helped to pray, "I renounce any way in which Satan is using my relationship with my aunt against me. I renounce anything she said or did to me, and anything she may have done on my behalf. And I thank You, Lord, that I am not a victim of those experiences. I am a child of God and free to be the person You created me to be."

Another woman had been led into a life of prostitution by her mother. She remembered that at a very young age a fortune-teller said to her, "Honey, you have a beautiful face and body. That will help you make it through life." She was led to renounce that false prophet and the lies that she should use her appearance and body to make it through life. Then she was encouraged to announce the truth that her body is a temple of the Holy Spirit and that God would supply all her needs.[55] Whenever you renounce a lie or any counterfeit experience, you should also affirm the truth and the Christian practices that enable you to live free in Christ.

# CHAPTER THREE
## OVERCOMING DECEPTION

Julie didn't just ask for an appointment to go through the Steps, she pursued it! As the session began, it didn't take long to find out why. With deep emotion, she told the story of her troubled life: a violent alcoholic father, sexual molestation, pornography, demonic experiences in her room, and exploitation by legalistic controllers at her church.

She earnestly worked through Step One on false guidance, which added to her composure as she went through Step Two. At the completion of this Step a wonderful thing happened. After reading through the Doctrinal Affirmation, she put her book down, and tears welled up in her eyes. Overwhelmed with the truth of who God is and who she is in Christ, she said, "Wow! That is soooo great!"

## TRUTH LIBERATES

Our Lord had just partaken of His last supper with His disciples before He walked to the cross. He knew His destiny, and He was about to leave behind 11 of the chosen 12 apostles, who would have to face opposition from the god of this world and continue the work Christ had begun. Satan had already deceived Judas, one of the disciples, into betraying Christ.

Jesus turned to the Father and prayed, "I do not ask Thee to take them out of the world, but to keep them from the evil one" (John 17:15). His prayer revealed how this freedom can be accomplished. "Sanctify them in the truth; Thy word is truth" (v. 17).

Believing the truth about who Christ is, why He came, and who we are in Him is the basis for our freedom. Knowing the truth set forth in God's Word is the mark of a true disciple. "If you abide in My word, then you are truly disciples of Mine; and you shall know the truth, and the truth shall make you free."[56]

> Knowing the truth is our first line of defense against the father of lies.

Knowing the truth is our first line of defense against the father of lies.[57] We acknowledge this truth in the inner self,[58] because a genuine faith is more than just intellectual assent or the accumulation of knowledge. God's truth must penetrate the heart, the very core of our beings. Only then will His truth bring freedom and lasting change in the inner person.

## THE NEED FOR HONESTY

We have been called to speak the truth in love and walk in the light, which means that our lives should be transparent before God and others. Anything less and we are living a lie. David was living a lie when he covered up his sin with Bathsheba, and he suffered greatly. He finally found freedom by acknowledging the truth. He wrote, "How blessed is the man . . . in whose spirit there is no deceit!"[59]

People caught in the bondage of sin lie. Bulimics lie about their binging and purging. Alcoholics hide their addictions and secretly stash bottles around the house. Sex addicts can keep their sin hidden for years. The first step in recovery is to get out of denial and face the truth. The only thing a Christian must admit to is the truth. "If we say that we have fellowship with Him and yet walk in the darkness, we lie and do not practice the truth; but if we walk in the light as He Himself is in the light, we have fellowship with one another, and the blood of Jesus His Son cleanses us from all sin."[60]

**Truth is never the enemy; it is always a liberating friend.**

The primary reason Julie, the girl in the story, found so much resolution is that she held nothing back. She was ready to walk in the light and speak the truth. She found forgiveness, cleansing, and freedom. Truth is never the enemy; it is always a liberating friend. Jesus is the perfect embodiment of truth, the liberating light, the best friend a man or woman could ever have. In Him there is no darkness at all. Jesus is the truth, and He sets honest people free.

## SATAN IS THE DECEIVER

Jesus described Satan as the father of lies. "Whenever he speaks a lie, he speaks from his own nature; for he is a liar, and the father of lies."[61] He cannot speak from truth because there is no truth in him. He can distort the truth, and he will even quote Scripture as he did when he tempted Jesus.

Satan keeps people in bondage by deceiving them and by blinding the minds of the unbelieving.[62] The power of Satan is in the lie, and the battle is for the mind. If he is able to deceive Christians into believing a lie, they will be spiritually impotent. He can't do anything about our identity and position in Christ, but if he can get us to believe it is not true, we will live as though it isn't. When the lies are exposed, Satan's power over the believer is broken.

Asking the Lord to reveal the deception and declaring the truth in the Doctrinal Affirmation at the conclusion of this Step is a powerful experience for many who have been deceived for years. Some will become increasingly confident as they verbalize the truth. You may struggle just trying to read through the Doctrinal Affirmation, but when you have completed the Steps, come back and read it again, and you will see the difference.

Most Christians honestly desire to live righteous lives but have distorted concepts of God and are ignorant of their position and identity in Christ. As you make this public declaration of faith, you are choosing God's truth about His nature, character and redemptive plan for your life.

## STANDING AGAINST THE DECEPTION

The battle is for the mind, and Satan will twist Scripture or tell half-truths in order to deceive us. So we must trust God to expose the deceit, remembering that the weapons we fight with are not the weapons of the world. On the contrary, they have divine power to demolish strongholds. In this Step, we use truth to "demolish arguments and every pretension that sets itself up against the knowledge of God, and we take captive every thought to make it obedient to Christ."[63]

> Freedom doesn't come from swatting flies (demons), it comes from taking out the garbage (sin).

During this Step a lady suddenly said, "Do you know what I'm hearing now? It's just a thought! That's all it is! I don't have to believe that trash anymore." She understood what the battle was, and it no longer had a hold over her. Another lady printed up a bunch of cards and was handing them out to anyone who wanted one. Each card contained the following questions, "Where did that thought come from? A loving God?"

If the voices, noises or laughter in your mind seems too overwhelming, stop and pray as you did at the beginning of these Steps on Page 33. You maintain control by exposing the lies and the battle for the mind, and by ignoring the distractions and continuing on with the Steps. Freedom doesn't come from swatting flies (demons), it comes from taking out the garbage (sin). The way we overcome the father of lies is by choosing the truth. We are not called to dispel the darkness; we are called to turn on the light. The freedom progressively comes by resolving the conflicts. The noise in your head is just an attempt by the enemy to get you off the path that leads to freedom. If you seemingly can't go on, then pray out loud: "I renounce this attack on me, and announce that my body is a temple of the Holy Spirit, and I choose to continue to seek my freedom."

Marcy was a sincere Christian who was being mentally "beaten up" with lies and accusations. She had been deceived into thinking that God was not a good God, that she couldn't trust Him, that she would never be free from her past. This fragile lady was slowly and gently guided through the Steps, renouncing all the lies as they surfaced. A few days later, she wrote:

God is different from what my concept of Him has been, and I choose to trust how God has revealed

Himself in the person of Jesus. I am His child, and I choose to believe that He will relate to me as a good Father would. I am a new person. This day is new, and I eagerly await to experience it as a new creation, free from my past.

# GOING THROUGH STEP TWO

In Step One you dealt with counterfeit guidance. In Step Two you will determine if you have been deceived. Scripture teaches that Christians can fall away from the faith by paying attention to deceiving spirits.[64] We can also be deceived by the world, deceive ourselves, and wrongly defend ourselves. We need God's help to determine whether deception has occurred, so ask for God's guidance as follows:

> *Dear Heavenly Father, You are the truth, and I desire to live by faith according to Your truth. The truth will set me free, but in many ways I have been deceived by the father of lies, the philosophies of this fallen world, and I have deceived myself. I choose to walk in the light, knowing that You love and accept me just as I am. As I consider areas of possible deception, I invite the Spirit of truth to guide me into all truth. Please protect me from all deception as You "search me, O God, and know my heart; try me and know my anxious thoughts; and see if there be any hurtful way in me, and lead me in the everlasting way" (Psalm 139:23, 24). In the name of Jesus I pray. Amen.*

Prayerfully consider the lists in the three exercises below, using the prayers at the end of each exercise in order to confess any ways you have given in to deception or wrongly defended yourself. You cannot instantly renew your mind, but the process will never get started without acknowledging mental strongholds or defense mechanisms, which are sometimes called mental flesh patterns.

## *Ways you can be deceived by the world:*

- ❏ Believing that acquiring money and things will bring lasting happiness. (Matthew 13:22; 1 Timothy 6:10)
- ❏ Believing that excessive food and alcohol can relieve my stress and make me happy. (Proverbs 23:19-21)
- ❏ Believing that an attractive body and personality will get me what I need. (Proverbs 31:10; 1 Peter 3:3, 4)
- ❏ Believing that gratifying sexual lust will bring lasting satisfaction. (Ephesians 4:22; 1 Peter 2:11)
- ❏ Believing that I can sin and get away without any negative consequences. (Hebrews 3:12, 13)
- ❏ Believing that I need more than what God has given me in Christ. (2 Corinthians 11:2-4, 13-15)
- ❏ Believing that I can do whatever I want and no one can touch me. (Proverbs 16:18; Obadiah 3; 1 Peter 5:5)

❏ Believing that unrighteous people who refuse to accept Christ go to heaven anyway. (1 Corinthians 6:9-11)

❏ Believing that I can associate with bad company and not become corrupted. (1 Corinthians 15:33, 34)

❏ Believing that I can read, see, or listen to anything and not be corrupted. (Proverbs 4:23-27; Matthew 5:28)

❏ Believing that there are no consequences on earth for my sin. (Galatians 6:7, 8)

❏ Believing that I must gain the approval of certain people in order to be happy. (Galatians 1:10)

❏ Believing that I must measure up to certain standards in order to feel good about myself. (Galatians 3:2, 3; 5:1)

*Lord Jesus, I confess that I have been deceived by* (confess the items you checked above). *I thank You for Your forgiveness, and I commit myself to believe only Your truth. In Jesus' name I pray.* **Amen.**

## Ways to deceive yourself:

❏ Hearing God's Word but not doing what it says. (James 1:22)

❏ Saying I have no sin. (1 John 1:8)

❏ Thinking I am something I'm really not. (Galatians 6:3)

❑ Thinking I am wise in this worldly age.
(1 Corinthians 3:18, 19)

❑ Thinking I can be truly religious but not bridle my tongue. (James 1:26)

❑ Thinking that God is the source of my problems. (Lamentations 3)

❑ Thinking I can live my life without the help of anyone else. (1 Corinthians 12:14-20)

*Lord Jesus, I confess that I have deceived myself by* (confess the items checked above). *Thank You for Your forgiveness. I commit myself to believe only Your truth. In Jesus' name I pray.* **Amen.**

## Ways to wrongly defend yourself:

❑ Denial of reality conscious or unconscious

❑ Fantasy
(escaping reality by daydreaming, TV, movies, music, computer, or video games, drugs, alcohol)

❑ Emotional insulation
(withdrawing from people or keeping people at a distance to avoid rejection)

❑ Regression
(reverting back to less threatening times)

❑ Displaced anger
(taking out frustrations on innocent people)

❑ Projection
(attributing to another what you find unacceptable in yourself)

- ❏ Rationalization
  (making excuses for my own poor behavior)
- ❏ Lying
  (protecting self through falsehoods)
- ❏ Blaming myself
  (when not responsible) and others
- ❏ Hypocrisy
  (presenting a false image)

*Lord Jesus, I confess that I have wrongly defended myself by* (confess the items checked above). *Thank You for Your forgiveness. I trust You to defend and protect me. In Jesus' name I pray.* **Amen.**

The wrong ways we have employed to shield ourselves from pain and rejection are often deeply engrained in our lives. You may need additional discipling or counseling to learn how to allow Christ to be your rock, fortress, deliverer, and refuge. The more you learn how loving, powerful, and protective God is, the more you will trust Him. The more you realize His complete acceptance of you in Christ, the more you'll be released to be open, honest, and vulnerable (in a healthy way) before God and others.

**True biblical faith, therefore, is choosing to believe and act upon what is true, because God has said it is true, and He is the Truth.**

The New Age movement has twisted the concept of faith by teaching that we make something true by believing it. That is false. We cannot create reality with our minds; only God can bring something out of nothing into existence. Our responsibility is to face reality and choose to believe what God says is true. True biblical faith, therefore, is choosing to believe and act upon what is true, because God has said it is true, and He is the Truth. Faith is something you decide to do, not something you feel like doing. Believing something doesn't make it true; it's already true, therefore we choose to believe it! Truth is not conditioned by whether we choose to believe it or not.

Everybody lives by faith. The only difference between Christian faith and non-Christian faith is the object of our faith. If the object of our faith is not trustworthy, then no amount of believing will change that. That's why our faith must be grounded on the solid rock of God's perfect, unchanging character and the truth of His word. For two thousand years Christians have known the importance of verbally, and publicly declaring truth. Read aloud the following Statements of Truth, and carefully consider what you are professing. You may find it helpful to read the words aloud daily for several weeks, which will help renew your mind to the truth.

## *Doctrinal Affirmation*

1. I recognize that there is only one true and living God who exists as the Father, Son, and Holy Spirit. He is worthy of all honor, praise, and glory as the One who made all things and holds all things together. (See Exodus 20:2, 3; Colossians 1:16, 17.)

2. I recognize that Jesus Christ is the Messiah, the Word who became flesh and dwelt among us. I believe that He came to destroy the works of the devil, and that He disarmed the rulers and authorities and made a public display of them, having triumphed over them. (See John 1:1, 14; Colossians 2:15; 1 John 3:8.)

3. I believe that God demonstrated His own love for me in that while I was still a sinner, Christ died for me. I believe that He has delivered me from the domain of darkness and transferred me to His kingdom, and in Him I have redemption, the forgiveness of sins. (See Romans 5:8; Col. 1:13, 14.)

4. I believe that I am now a child of God and that I am seated with Christ in the heavenlies. I believe that I was saved by the grace of God through faith, and that it was a gift and not a result of any works on my part. (See Ephesians 2:6, 8, 9; 1 John 3:1-3.)

5. I choose to be strong in the Lord and in the strength of His might. I put no confidence in the flesh, for the weapons of warfare are not of the flesh but are divinely powerful for the destruction of strongholds. I put on the full armor of God. I resolve to stand firm in my faith and resist the evil one. (See 2 Corinthians 10:4; Ephesians 6:10-20; Philippians 3:3.)

6. I believe that apart from Christ I can do nothing, so I declare my complete dependence on Him. I choose to abide in Christ in order to bear much fruit and glorify my Father. I announce to Satan that Jesus is my Lord. I reject any and all counterfeit gifts or works of Satan in my life. (See John 15:5, 8; 1 Corinthians 12:3.)

7. I believe that the truth will set me free and that Jesus is the truth. If He sets me free, I will be free indeed. I recognize that walking in the light is the only path of true fellowship with God and man. Therefore, I stand against all of Satan's deception by taking every thought captive in obedience to Christ. I declare that the Bible is the only authoritative standard for truth and life. (See John 8:32,36; 14:6; 2 Corinthians 10:5; 2 Timothy 3:15-17; 1 John 1:3-7.)

8. I choose to present my body to God as a living and holy sacrifice and the members of my body as instruments of righteousness. I choose to

renew my mind by the living Word of God in order that I may prove that the will of God is good, acceptable, and perfect. I put off the old self with its evil practices and put on the new self. I declare myself to be a new creation in Christ. (See Romans 6:13; 12:1, 2; 2 Corinthians 5:17; Colossians 3:9, 10.)

9. By faith, I choose to be filled with the Spirit so that I can be guided into all truth. I choose to walk by the Spirit so that I will not carry out the desires of the flesh. (See John 16:13; Galatians 5:16; Ephesians 5:18.)

10. I renounce all selfish goals and choose the ultimate goal of love. I choose to obey the two greatest commandments: to love the Lord my God with all my heart, soul, mind, and strength and to love my neighbor as myself. (See Matthew 22:37-39; 1 Timothy 1:5)

11. I believe that the Lord Jesus has all authority in heaven and on earth, and He is the head over all rule and authority. I am complete in Him. I believe that Satan and his demons are subject to me in Christ since I am a member of Christ's body. Therefore, I obey the command to submit to God and resist the devil, and I command Satan in the name of Jesus Christ to leave my presence. (See Matthew 28:18; Ephesians 1:19-23; Colossians 2:10; James 4:7)

There is no way that we can instantly renew our minds. Defense mechanisms and flesh patterns have been learned over time and they have to be unlearned, which will take time. The purpose in this Step is to identify the ways you have been deceived and expose unhealthy ways of thinking and believing. It reveals where you need to grow. You are not hopeless, and you don't need someone else to do your thinking and believing for you. Such lies have been played over and over again in people's minds. You must assume responsibility for choosing the truth, regardless of how your emotions feel.

> **You must assume responsibility for choosing the truth, regardless of how your emotions feel.**

Suppose there is a dirt road leading to your house in the country. If you continually drive over that road the same exact way, ruts will be formed over time. The sun will dry those ruts and make them hard as concrete. The easiest thing is to allow the car to drift along in those ruts. It will be a rough ride compared to the smooth ride that you could have on the surface right beside the ruts. You will immediately feel the resistance on the wheel to return to the ruts in the road when you only make a half-hearted effort to steer out of them.

If you want to get out of the rut, you will have to be totally committed and willing to make deliberate choices.

In the same way, if you no longer want to be controlled by the strongholds or "rut thinking" that the world, the flesh and the devil has put in your mind over years, you need to be committed to breaking those strongholds and make deliberate choices based on the truth of God's Word. You choose; you don't passively let your old patterns of thinking decide. You take every thought captive in obedience to Christ and choose His truth. This is how we renew our minds—by knowing and choosing the truth, and by letting the Word of Christ richly dwell within us. (See Romans 12:2; Philippians 4:8; Colossians 3:16.)

## EXPOSING LIES AND AFFIRMING TRUTH

A lady wrote, "Going through the Steps to Freedom has been the most exciting part of my Christian walk." She had struggled with voices and screaming in her head, nightmares and apparitions in her room, and strong deception through lies and condemnation. She said, "I have been unwilling to take responsibility for my own thoughts. I have wanted some kind of help from the outside without being willing to do the necessary work myself." In a letter she wrote to Jesus, she said, "I confess my unbelief, my selfishness, my obsessive thoughts. I renounce the lies that would destroy and incapacitate me. I ask Your forgiveness and forsake all thinking that would destroy the truth that is in me." Attached to her letter were six typewritten pages of lies she had believed, accompanied by Scripture verses she found that exposed those lies and affirmed the truth.

The same woman wrote this letter after going through the Steps to Freedom:

As I've thought about and weighed what happened in God's presence in your office, I am awestruck at the reality that not only has Christ completely severed the spiritual bond between myself and all the others I was involved with, but that He also touched the deeper issue—a place where I have held the belief that I actually became the slut, whore, adulterer, the "evil one," the "witch" that mom and dad had always said I was.

Facing the reality of that truth—or rather the lies that I have believed about myself—has been more than I ever believed God could make clean or redeem. I could not escape the embarrassment, nor could I forgive my willing participation. The violations were easier to renounce because I was not choosing them for myself.

Is it possible that as I've continued to renounce both the sexual acts themselves and the beliefs that I became the embodiment of the evil I participated in, that the Lord would expunge the record...and change my life...that I am no longer identified by the names my earthly father gave me, but I am truly a new person in Christ...that I am as you said, "clean as a hound's tooth?" I have always thought of myself as a slut and an adulteress who was just taking up space in the Church, but who could never take a position of responsibility or ministry because my past is so evil.

It's like God has taken a giant sponge to the battered and bloody portion of my life that has been a major stronghold, absorbed all the blood, all the pain, all the lies. And as He took all this away, He left me new and free and clean in Him. I don't have to contend with the weight of that sin because it's forgiven, nailed to the cross through the blood of Jesus.

I have known all the lies in my head and have wanted to believe that God's Word was true; today I know it in my heart and spirit. As I renounced these things, I thought, How can these words set me free? Yet how could they not? They are the power of God.

Today, I don't just believe God is cleansing me; I know I'm clean! I don't just believe God will free me from my past; I know I'm free! I am no longer my father's daughter, his sex toy. I am no longer another man's mistress. I am no longer the embodiment of the evil I participated in. I am a child of the King, called and chosen by Him. Cleansed, forgiven, made new to live in His family forever. Free to love and give and enter into relationship with Him and the Church, to be the person He has called me to be. Praise His name!

# Chapter Four
## Overcoming the Bondage of Bitterness

Those who have truly helped others experience their freedom in Christ will testify that forgiveness of others is the primary issue that needs to be resolved. Unforgiveness by Christians affords Satan his greatest access to the Church, and many believers are bound to the past because they have failed to forgive others as Christ has forgiven them.

## WHY SOME PEOPLE RESIST FORGIVENESS

Some people react negatively to the idea of forgiving others, because they see it as another form of victimization. It goes against their sense of justice. "Oh, sure, just forgive and keep getting slapped around!" They believe it is a sign of weakness, a continuation of the sickening saga of codependency.

On the contrary, forgiveness is a courageous act that reflects the grace of God. Forgiveness is not tolerating sin. God forgives, but He doesn't tolerate sin. Therefore, scriptural boundaries must be set up to stop further abuse. Forgiving others is something you do for your sake, and resistance breaks down when you understand what it is and how to do it.

> Forgiving others is something you do for your sake...

Some don't want to forgive because they want revenge. Seeking revenge is letting the devil set the agenda. It puts you on the same level as the abuser and usurps God's role of exacting justice. Paul writes, "Never take your own revenge, beloved, but leave room for the wrath of God, for it is written, 'Vengeance is Mine, I will repay,' says the Lord."[65] Some people just want the soul satisfaction of hating the wretch. But hanging on to bitterness only sickens the soul. Trying to cover it up doesn't fool anyone, least of all ourselves, because "the heart knows its own bitterness."[66]

Nobody is denying that you have been hurt, and some of you have been hurt badly. After helping hundreds work through their painful memories of unspeakable atrocities, my heart goes out to victims in ways I can hardly explain. Working with abused people has left me close to tears all the time. After hearing hundreds of stories, I still can hardly believe what people are capable of doing to one another.

I went through a soul-searching time in the early days of this ministry. I didn't want to hear any more horrible stories. In fact, I don't think I could hear them today if I didn't see resolution. What keeps me going is the freedom that comes when people work through

**...there is an answer for wounded people.**

the Steps and forgive from their hearts. I thank God that there is an answer for wounded people.

I have said to hundreds of people in counseling sessions and I am saying it to you, "I'm so sorry that happened to you." Instead of having a father who would protect and provide for you, you had a father who abused you physically, verbally, and sexually. Instead of having a mother who would comfort and encourage you, you had a mother who verbally abused you. Instead of having a pastor who would shepherd you, you had a legalistic man who tried to control you under a cloud of condemnation. What you thought would be a safe date, turned out to be date rape.

The vast majority of the victimizers will never come back and ask for forgiveness. They won't even acknowledge they did anything wrong. That makes forgiveness harder, because the victim believes the perpetrators got away with something. You may be suffering the consequences of some abuser's sin, and that person won't even acknowledge that they have sinned. To all female readers I want to acknowledge and apologize for the way we men have looked at you as sex objects, and for the way we have touched you and violated you. As a father, husband, and a man, I'm asking for your forgiveness. Would you forgive us men? It is not your fault. You did not deserve it. It is our sickness. As a father and grandfather, I want to ask all those who are reading this book to forgive us fathers who never hugged you, protected you, and believed in you. Would you forgive us -- for your sake?

# BEGINNING STEP THREE

Let me encourage you to ask God who it is that you need to forgive and then I will explain what forgiveness is and how you can do it. In the following prayer, all you are asking for are the names of the people you need to forgive.

> *Dear Heavenly Father, I thank You for the riches of Your kindness, forbearance, and patience, knowing that Your kindness has led me to repentance* (Romans 2:4). *I confess that I have not extended that same patience and kindness toward those who have hurt or offended me. Instead I have held on to my anger, bitterness, and resentment toward them.*

*Please bring to my mind all the people I need to forgive in order that I may do so. In Jesus' name I pray.* **Amen.**

## MAKING THE LIST

When you have finished praying, write down on a piece of paper every name that comes to your mind. About ninety percent of the time, mother and father are mentioned first. The first few names that come to your mind are usually the people who contributed to your greatest source of pain. Some may be tempted to think, "There isn't anybody I need to forgive."

> When you forgive, you set the captive free, only to realize that you were the captive.

That is highly unlikely since we have all suffered at the hands of someone else. Write down the names that are coming to your mind right now. The Lord wants you to live a liberated life in Him, but you can't if you are bound to the past in bitterness. He has commanded you to forgive for your sake, so He will bring to mind both the people and the events that you are chained to in unforgiveness. When you forgive, you set the captive free, only to realize that you were the captive. Who are the relatives you need to forgive? Teachers? Employers? Friends? Co-workers? Church leaders?"

## DEALING WITH SELF AND GOD

The two most overlooked names are: "yourself" and "God." In many cases, anger toward self or God is greater than anger toward any other person. The devil capitalizes on our ignorance of God and His ways and on our irresponsibility by pummeling us with thoughts such as, God isn't going to help you. He doesn't love you. How can you be a Christian and do the things you do? Look how weak and helpless you are. People who struggle with such thoughts are angry at themselves and/or God, and are disillusioned by the Christian life.

The concept of "letting go" of anger, guilt, and condemnation toward self is something many have never considered. Those feelings are rooted in our failure to understand God's cleansing and forgiveness. Only God can forgive our sins, which separate us from Him, and He has. But we need to forgive ourselves for our failures, for letting God down, and for hurting others. Otherwise we believe the subtle deception that we must atone for our own sins.

Believers paralyzed by condemnation are being victimized by the accuser of the brethren (Satan), or by their own faulty consciences, rather than the truth of God's grace. The latter is psychological guilt based on years of performance-based living and legalistic religious beliefs. These kinds of people live as though Christ's death was not sufficient to cover their sins. You can hang on the cross if you want to, but it won't do you any good. The Apostle Paul warned us when he said, "Let no one keep defrauding you of your prize by delighting in self-abasement."[67]

You are not being presumptuous by forgiving yourselves, because you are not accomplishing forgiveness from God. Only God can forgive our sins through His Son. Forgiving ourselves is actually receiving forgiveness from God. Forgiving ourselves is saying in effect, "Lord, I believe that You have forgiven me and cleansed me of my sins. Because of Your great love and grace—not because I deserve it—I choose to no longer condemn myself when You have forgiven me. I receive Your forgiveness and cleansing."

## RELEASING BITTERNESS TOWARD GOD

Bitterness toward God is far more common than most people would care to admit. But when they become honest about their anger toward God, another stronghold begins to crumble. They believe God has been unfair and let them down...by failing to answer an important prayer...by allowing them to suffer and not rescuing them...by not endowing them with certain blessings, looks, gifts, abilities, success or, financial security.

Obviously, God doesn't need to be forgiven, because He cannot commit any sin of commission or omission. But we need to destroy "speculations and every lofty thing raised up against the knowledge of God" and take "every thought captive to the obedience of Christ."[68] Satan's scheme is to turn us against God by raising up thoughts against Him. These deceptive thoughts often sound like: God doesn't love me. He isn't going to do anything to help me. They cause us to rebel against His Lordship. Satan is defeated when we release God from our own false expectations and stop blaming Him for our own failures and the failure of the Church to adequately equip the saints so they can live a liberated life in Christ.

People don't always forgive others because of what others did to them; people forgive others for what they think others have done to them. Bitterness isn't always rooted in reality. It is rooted in their perceptions. Some people put their pastor's name on their lists for silly reasons like not answering the phone when they called. But the pastor wasn't home or he would've answered the phone! The pastor didn't do anything wrong, but the person thought he did, so the person needed to forgive him. Roots of bitterness spring up and many are defiled,[69] because of misunderstandings.

## THOUGHTS RAISED UP AGAINST GOD

That is why it is not blasphemous to "forgive" God -- because the bitterness is not based in reality but in thoughts raised up against the knowledge of Him. God understands that concept much better than we do because

He alone knows the thoughts and intentions of our hearts. The only way to overcome bitterness is to forgive.

When people have worked through their bitterness toward God, they immediately acknowledge the fact that God hasn't done anything wrong. It won't help you to overcome your bitterness toward God by defending Him. First of all, God doesn't need to be defended. Second, forgiveness starts where people are at. Telling others they shouldn't feel the way they do toward God or anyone else is futile. They can't change the way they feel. We've participated in a subtle form of rejection when we won't accept or acknowledge their frustration and pain. If you find "forgiving" God uncomfortable, or if you think it is absolutely wrong, then you might try praying, "Lord, I know You haven't done anything wrong, but I want to repent of the anger I have against You for...." Angry feelings must be dealt with, or it won't do much good to go on, because God is your only hope.

Most people won't submit to God if they are bitter toward Him or think they can't trust Him. I can only tell you from experience that working through the bitterness toward God brings tremendous healing and restoration. Job is a good example of a believer who repented of anger toward God: "Therefore I retract, and I repent in dust and ashes."[70] Forgiving others is not a self-righteous activity nor a blaming exercise. It is a humbling and healing experience that faces the hurt and the hate, and then chooses the way of the Cross.

## GIVING UP OUR RIGHT TO BLAME

Some people deal with their emotional pain by pointing fingers. "That person violated me" or "I'm suffering because of that person." While that may be true, it doesn't resolve the problem. Blaming someone else can be a cover for your own guilt, or it reveals a heart that is more prone to seek revenge than to forgive.

To place the blame on somebody else can be nothing more than an excuse to stay in the bondage of bitterness. The reason that many still feel the emotional pain from the past is because they haven't forgiven. I can empathize with these people because they have been hurt. But I also care enough to help them realize that bad things happen to good people all the time, and it may happen to them again. I can't guarantee that a woman will not be sexually assaulted, but I can say that God has a means by which that event doesn't have to control her for the rest of her life. Nobody can fix your past, but by the grace of God you can be free from it.

> Nobody can fix your past, but by the grace of God you can be free from it.

Forgiveness is an act of the will whereby we give up our claim to seek revenge for an offense against us. God could have justifiably exercised His wrath against us and all mankind. Instead, "He made Him who knew no sin to be sin on our behalf, that we might become the righteousness of God in Him."[71] Was it difficult for Jesus to accept His Father's will? He said to Peter, James, and John, "My soul is deeply grieved, to the point of death,"[72] and He cried out, "My Father, if it is possible, let this cup pass from Me; yet not as I will, but as Thou wilt." The will of our heavenly Father was that Jesus go to the cross, but the grace of God was incredibly evident even in His hour of agony. As Jesus looked down upon those who would crucify Him, He said, "Father, forgive them; for they do not know what they are doing."[73]

> Forgiveness is an act of the will whereby we give up our claim to seek revenge for an offense against us.

The Cross reveals the cost of forgiveness and the pain of bearing the penalty of someone else's sin. At the Cross, Jesus died once for all the sins of the world.[74] He paid the penalty for my sins, your sins, and all the sins committed by others against all the people of this world. The victim cries out, "Where is the justice?" It's in the Cross. Forgiving others would be a moral outrage without the Cross.

In the same manner that God has forgiven us, God wants us to forgive others. "Let all bitterness and wrath and anger and clamor and slander be put away from you, along with all malice. And be kind to one another, tenderhearted, forgiving each other, just as God in Christ also has forgiven you."[75] When you face the reality of forgiving others, know that the grace of God will always enable you to do the will of God.

Many Christians try to forgive over and over again, but still feel hurt and confused. They haven't understood how to forgive from the heart, or they haven't finished all the Steps, and the process isn't complete without doing that. Forgiving from our hearts is part of submitting to God, but it will take the rest of the Steps before they are fully ready to resist the devil. People win a major battle going through this Step, but complete freedom doesn't usually come until the last Step.

## GIVE SATAN NO ADVANTAGE

One of the most definitive teachings on forgiveness is in Matthew 18:21-35. Several issues stand out in this passage. First, we are to continue forgiving no matter how many times we have been sinned against. Second, the degree that we have been forgiven by God is far greater than the degree we will ever have to forgive others. Third, repayment is impossible. Fourth, we are to forgive from our hearts or suffer the consequences of being tormented by the accuser of the brethren. If we will not forgive as we have been forgiven, our heavenly Father will hand us over to the torturers (see verses 34&35). That's not because He doesn't love us; that's because He doesn't want us to live in the bondage of bitterness. He wants us to live free and productive lives in Christ. God disciplines those He loves.

Paul warns us about Satan's entrapment when there is unforgiveness: "Whom you forgive anything, I forgive also; for indeed what I have forgiven, if I have forgiven anything, I did it for your sakes in the presence of Christ, in order that no advantage be taken of us by Satan; for we are not ignorant of his schemes [thoughts]."[76] We are not to sin through anger, because that gives the devil an opportunity as well.[77]

## Justice, Mercy, and Grace

Consider these simple definitions of justice, mercy and grace as they apply to relationships: Justice is giving people what they deserve. If God were perfectly just in dealing with us, we would all go to hell. God is a just God, and "The wages of sin is death."[78]

Mercy is not giving people what they deserve. "But when the kindness of God our Savior and His love for mankind appeared, He saved us, not on the basis of deeds which we have done in righteousness, but according to His mercy."[79] Justice had to be served, so Jesus took upon Himself the wrath of God.

Grace is giving us what we don't deserve. "For by grace you have been saved through faith."[80] Forgiveness and eternal life are free gifts from God.

So the Lord instructs us to, "Be merciful, just as your Father is merciful."[81] We are not to give people what they deserve (be merciful); we are to give them what they don't deserve (be gracious). We are called to love people, not because they are lovable or deserve to be loved, but because we have become "partakers of the divine nature."[82] God loves us because it is His nature to love us. "God is love."[83] "By this all men will know that you are My disciples, if you have love for one another."[84] This ability to love one another is possible only by the grace of God, as is the ability to forgive as we have been forgiven.

The most common Greek word in the New Testament translated to forgive basically means to send away or to let go. In forgiving, we send away the devil so he can't torment us, and we let go of the past so it can no longer have a hold on us. The pain and anger is released as we forgive from our hearts.

## WHAT TO AVOID

Two major errors are to be avoided when addressing the issue of forgiveness. The first is more common among counselors. Influenced by secular resources, some counselors teach that forgiveness is a process and tell many that they are not ready to forgive. They tell people they have to go through all the painful memories first and then they will be able to

> We forgive in order to heal.

forgive. The problem is they will never get there. Rehearsing the painful memories week after week only deepens the wounds and reinforces the abuse. The implication is that one has to heal in order to forgive, but in actuality, it is the other way around. We forgive in order to heal.

...forgiveness is agreeing to live with the consequences of another person's sins.

The other error is more common in the Church. The extreme version would sound like this: "You shouldn't feel that way; you just need to forgive." They just bypassed forgiveness. We have to forgive from the heart. Forgiveness is a hard choice, which includes: (1) allowing God to surface the names of every offending person and painful memory; (2) agreeing to live with the consequences of the other person's sin without seeking revenge; and (3) letting God deal with the offending person in His way and in His time.

All forgiveness is efficacious or substitutionary. Christ paid the price for our sins, and we pay the price for those who sinned against us. In a practical sense, forgiveness is agreeing to live with the consequences of another person's sins. "But that isn't fair," some protest. Of course it isn't, but we will have to do so anyway. Everybody is living with the consequences of somebody else's sin. We are all living with the consequences of Adam's sin. We have the choice to live in the bondage of bitterness or in the freedom of forgiveness.

## GETTING TO THE EMOTIONAL CORE

As you pray through your list of names, stay with each individual until you are sure you have dealt with all the remembered pain—what he or she did, how he or she hurt you, how he or she made you feel (rejected, unloved, unworthy, dirty, etc.). This process is important because facing specific issues is what enables you to get to the emotional core, where the damage was done and the healing takes place. Forgiving superficially results in superficial freedom and healing.

Many people have sincerely tried to forgive but weren't able to because they didn't understand the real source of their bitterness and the subsequent lies they have believed about themselves. Feelings of abandonment would fit into this category. Forgiving someone for hurting you may only be dealing with the symptom. You may need to ask yourself, "What specifically happened to me?" "How did I respond at the time?" and "How has it affected me today?" Anger, sadness, and depression are only the emotional consequences of what happened.

Physical, emotional, spiritual, and sexual abuse can also severely damage your self-concept. Your identity becomes wrapped around the abuse. A rape victim may feel like a whore, and the emotionally battered person may feel worthless. Forgiving the person for making her feel like a whore or feeling worthless will not get it done. She would need to forgive like this: "I forgive that man who raped me, for forcing me to have sex with him against my will, and for violating my body, which is a temple of God, when I wanted to glorify God in my body. And I renounce the lie that I am a whore or that my body is dirty." (More will be said about this kind of renunciation in Step Six.) Or you may need to pray, "I forgive my mother for saying I will never amount to anything and for constantly putting me down by saying _____ (be specific), because it made me feel _____ (state how it made you feel, i.e. incompetent, inferior, worthless, etc.). I renounce the lies that I have believed about myself. I am not the terrible person my mother said I was; I am a child of God, and I choose to believe what God says about me."

Hurtful experiences in early childhood shape our self-perceptions. It is common to hear people tearfully pray: "Lord, I forgive my father (or mother) for beating me, for never caring about what was happening in my life, for not believing me when I told him about the sexual abuse. I forgive him for what he said and did that caused me to feel dirty, unloved, and worthless." Such negative programming contributes to a distorted sense of self. Forgiving others connects them to a loving Father who sees them as His children, cleansed by the blood of the Lamb.

Mental strongholds are torn down as people forgive those who have offended them. They have lived under the condemnation of those labels for years. For the liberated Christian, "There is now no condemnation for those who are in Christ Jesus."[85] Lies are exposed so they can live according to the truth of who they really are in Christ.

## PREPARING YOUR HEARTS

Bitterness is like swallowing poison and hoping the other person will die. It is to the soul what cancer is to the body. If you knew that you had a form of cancer that could be removed by surgery, wouldn't you say to the doctor, "Go for it! Get it all!"? Bitterness, like cancer, affects every part of your being. Forgiving from your heart those who have hurt you is God's way of removing the cancer.

> Bitterness is like swallowing poison and hoping the other person will die.

Tragically, this cancer of the soul is a communicable disease that can be spread to others. That is why the Word of God says, "See to it that no one misses the grace of God and that no bitter root grows up to cause trouble and defile many."[86] Entire families and churches can be defiled by roots of bitterness.

God may bring to mind offending people and experiences you have totally forgotten. Let Him do it even if it is painful. Remember, you are doing this for your sake. God wants you to be free. Don't rationalize or explain the offender's behavior. Forgiveness is dealing with your pain and leaving the other person to God. Positive feelings will follow in time; freeing yourself from the past is the critical issue right now.

Don't say, "Lord, please help me to forgive" because He is already helping you. Don't say, "Lord, I want to forgive" because you are bypassing the hard-core choice to forgive, which is your responsibility. Stay with each individual until you are sure you have dealt with all the remembered pain—what they did, how they hurt you, how they made you feel (rejected, unloved, unworthy, dirty, etc.).

Are you ready to forgive the people on your list so that you can be free in Christ and so that those people and your past no longer have any control over you? If you are ready, then for each person on your list pray aloud as follows:

Lord, I choose to forgive _____

(name the person) for _____

(what they did or failed to do), which made me feel

_____

(share the painful memories).

## AS THEY PRAY

One young lady said, "I can't forgive my mother. I hate her!" Now she can! The Lord isn't asking you to like those who have offended you. You can't deny or play with your emotions that way. The Lord wants you to forgive so you can put a stop to the pain you have experienced.

Some are reluctant to forgive others for the wrongs they have done because they think they are judging people by forgiving them. When a young anorexic girl came to her father on the list, she said, "I feel like I need to ask him to forgive me." I told her, "Maybe you do, but that is not what we are dealing with here. We are dealing with your pain."

Sometimes people are torn between feelings of love and loyalty for their parents and the need to face the pain they caused. Forgiving your parents for being something less than perfect is not condemning them. We do not blame our parents for their imperfections; they had parents who were imperfect, too. But facing the truth and forgiving your parents is what stops the cycle of abuse that continues on from one generation to another.

As you work through your list, make sure you stay with each person until you have dealt with every painful memory that God brings to your mind. Many people have tried to shove these painful memories down into their subconscious. Such suppression is considered a conscious denial. Others cannot honestly recall what happened to them. The Lord has allowed that to happen. The pain was too great to deal with at the time, so the Lord has made it possible for them to dissociate. He will reveal it at a later time when there is enough maturity, adequate support, and the means to resolve it. The Lord frequently brings back repressed memories during this process. Some attempt to deal with their pain by denying that anything bad ever happened or by pretending that it didn't really bother them. Denial and cover-up are never God's way.

## EMOTIONS VARY

Forgiving from the heart will be an emotional catharsis for many, while others may remain emotionally blocked and unable to feel anything. A missionary lady looked at her list and slowly pushed it away. Then she pulled it back, and then pushed it away again. She said, "My counselor has been trying to get me to cry for three months." I had said nothing about crying. Finally, she took the list and started with the first name. "Lord, I forgive..." and collapsed in tears. Years of emotional pain surfaced as she forgave one person after another.

Some may work through their lists rather stoically. That is because people have different temperaments. Shedding tears is not the only way of expressing grief and pain. Some consciously and deliberately come to terms with their abuses and painfully choose to forgive from their hearts without shedding a tear. However, you may have never identified the true sources of your pain. Ask yourself, "How did that make you feel at the time?" or "When you think about it now, how does it make you feel now?" You may experience a flood of emotions unleashed. Some may forgive without showing any emotion until they come to a particular name, and then the release comes.

# FACING THE PAIN AND MOVING ON

The primary objective is to face the truth, acknowledge the pain, forgive the offenders and move on. For many, this may be the first time they have ever acknowledged, understood or faced the root of their pain. Allow yourself to experience the pain and express your emotions. You may have chosen to stuff your feelings and live in denial for the fear of that happening, but that is exactly what must happen. You can't be right with God and not be real.

Some people were taught not to express their emotions, especially negative ones. "Real men don't cry," they have been told, or "Being emotionally expressive is wrong and a sign of weakness." Were you ever told that it was wrong or weak to express your emotions? What happened to you when you were emotionally honest in your home? Do you believe it is wrong to be emotionally honest? To be free in Christ, you must forgive those who trained you and renounce the lies you have been taught concerning your emotional nature. The one who is free in Christ will be emotionally free as well.

One woman had never been able to feel emotional sadness for herself but could weep for others. Her father had molested her when she was a child, and to guard his secret, he threatened her with more harm if she ever cried or told anyone. When this memory surfaced while going through forgiveness, she was encouraged to renounce the lie that she should not feel her own emotions and announce the truth that God created her with the emotional ability to experience joy, sorrow, laughter, and tears. As she did that, a tear began to form in the corner of her eye. Immediately she began to weep, and she continued to sob for some time.

Some people are like bananas -- the peel is removed and all their problems are resolved the first time they go through the Steps. Not everyone, however, can cover their entire past in one session. Some are like onions. The first time through, they will take off the outer layer. They may feel a great sense of joy as though a weight has been lifted. They dealt with all they knew, but they may recall other things in the coming days. Now they will know what to do when painful memories surface or new offenses take place. You must resolve what you do know. If there is more, the Lord will surface it at the right time. When He does, there will always be someone to forgive and/or something to renounce.

## DEVELOP AN IDENTITY LIST

As you work through your list, it can be very helpful to make a "before and after" identity chart. Take a clean piece of paper and draw a line down the center of the page. At the top of the left column, write the words "Old Identity." Under that column write down every negative thing you said about yourself or was said about you. At the top of the right column, write "New Identity in Christ." Write down what is really true about yourself in Christ.

Recall the words that describe your beliefs about yourself as a result of abuse. In the left-hand column, record such words as: "dirty," "unloved," "abandoned," "not worth anything" and "can't do anything right." Especially record those words associated with the people of influence in your early years (mother, father, siblings, etc.). Such labels influenced your belief system and behavior patterns.

When you go to a store and buy a can or package of food off the shelf, it has a manufacturer's label describing the contents. As you go through life—the bad experiences, the things done to you, the things said to you, the wrong things you were involved in—Satan is there with paper and pencil writing a label for your life. Now that you are alive in Christ, you are no longer a product of your past; you are a product of the work of Christ on the cross. All the old labels of the world don't describe the contents of who you are anymore. Renounce the lies and choose the truth. Some examples are as follows:

▲ For those who have been betrayed by a parent and transferred that mistrust to their heavenly Father: "Lord, I renounce the lies I've believed about You because of the way my earthly father treated me. I announce the truth that You are not like my earthly father. You are perfectly loving and faithful."

▲ For those who think they are responsible for holding their dysfunctional families together and for being a parent's emotional support: "Lord, I renounce the lie that I am responsible for being a savior to the people around me or that I must always be responsible for others by being the strong one. Thank you, Lord, that it's all right for me to be honest about my own need. Thank you that when I am weak, You are strong within me." (See 2 Corinthians 12:9, TLB.)

▲ For those who have been constantly put down by the authority figures in their lives: "Lord, I renounce the lie that I am unworthy and insignificant. I announce the truth that I am your special child and I am precious to You." Or "Lord, I renounce the lie that I am a helpless victim as I felt when I was a child. I announce the truth that I can do all things through Christ who strengthens me." (See Philippians 4:13.)

## SEEKING FORGIVENESS FROM OTHERS

Some are reluctant to forgive others because they believe they have to go to those people. The prospect of facing their abusers is too traumatic to even consider. To forgive others, you only need to go to God. Don't confuse the issue of forgiving others with the need to ask for forgiveness, which is called for in Matthew 5:23-26. The Lord requires us to go to others before we go to Him and seek reconciliation if we know that someone has something against us.

The important thing to remember is that if we have hurt someone else, we need to go to that person first before we go to church. But if we have been hurt by others, we need to forgive them by going first to God. Forgiveness must precede reconciliation. Paul wrote, "If possible, so far as it depends upon you, be at peace with all men,"[87] but it doesn't always depend upon you. You cannot be reconciled with someone who doesn't want to be reconciled. The goal is for you to be free from past abuses and abusers. Reconciliation may come, but only if the abusers will own up to their abusive ways and honestly seek forgiveness. The freedom of the abused is never contingent upon whether the abuser will own up to it. You must be willing to forgive from your heart regardless of what the abusers do. If you make your willingness to forgive others contingent upon them, then you will be controlled by abusers all your life. You may protest, but you don't know how bad they hurt me. They are still hurting you. Forgiveness is how you stop the pain. Forgiving others from your heart is a draining experience, but a major conflict has been resolved between you and God. Satan has no right to torment you anymore. It is normal to feel exhausted, but a brief break, a good stretch, a glass of water, and you are ready to go on to the next Step. But before you do, finish this Step with the following prayer:

*Lord Jesus, I choose not to hold on to my resentment and bitterness. I relinquish my right to seek and revenge, and I ask You to heal my damaged emotions. Thank You for setting me free from the bondage of bitterness and free from my past experiences. I now ask You to bless those who have hurt me. In Jesus' name I pray. Amen.*

# Chapter Five
## OVERCOMING REBELLION

A young lady made an appointment with her pastor, hoping to resolve a relational issue in her family, but what surfaced during the Steps was an extremely abusive marriage that ended in divorce. She had remarried, but found herself in the same cycle of abuse. Her past training and the pressure of family and friends reinforced the false belief that submission is being passive to physical and emotional abuse. Her strategy for survival was crumbling as was her ability to cope.

Many like her spend their lives accommodating their abusers, hoping someday they will finally live up to their expectations and receive the acceptance and affirmation they believe they must have in order to be worthwhile people. However, ask yourself the question, "What if your mother, father, or spouse never accepted you or gave you the affirmation you believe you need?" That is a real possibility, but you don't have to have their approval if you know who you are in Christ, because the God of this universe has already accepted and affirmed you. Others decide to do the opposite and make a conscious choice to never be pushed around again by anyone, and they become rebellious. Both the rebel and the co-dependent must find their identity, acceptance, security, and significance in Christ and become the person God created them to be.

## WHO IS IN CONTROL?

Who would you say is in control of your life right now? Do you think you are? God never designed your soul to function as master. At any one moment, you are either serving "mammon" or God.[88] The poet says, "I am the master of my fate and the captain of my soul." Oh, no, he isn't! Self-seeking, self-serving, self-justifying, self-glorifying, and self-centered living are in actuality serving the world, the flesh, and the devil, being deceived into thinking we are serving self.

Denying ourselves is the way of the Cross. Saying no to ourselves and yes to God is the ultimate struggle in life. Believing we are God is the biggest lie of all. It originated in the garden when Satan said, "You will be like God."[89] Trying to be or play God is the biggest mistake we can make. It seems so sacrificial to surrender all to God, but what are you really sacrificing? You are sacrificing the lower life to gain the higher life. It is the great ambition of fallen humanity to be happy as animals instead of being blessed as children of God.

You are sacrificing the pleasure of things to gain the pleasure of life. What would you exchange for love, joy, peace, patience, kindness, goodness, faithfulness, gentleness and self-control? A new car? A better home? A higher position? The belief that those things will give you love, joy, and peace is the lie of the world, even though there is nothing inherently wrong with having degrees, titles, and physical possessions. You are sacrificing the temporal to gain the eternal. Some sacrifice! In reality, denying self-rule is the magnificent defeat. Only when we come to the end of our resources do we discover His resources. Lordship is not a negative doctrine. We are liberated in Christ when Jesus is Lord.

## LEARN TO TRUST GOD

Beth was raised in a legalistic church-going family. When she met and married Todd, who was a Christian, she fully expected that her life would be satisfying and that he would be able to meet all of her needs. Her fantasy faded as the marriage failed. Disillusioned and angry with her parents and husband, Beth developed a deep distrust of God. This attitude led to open rebellion and despair. She dabbled in false religions and adopted a worldly lifestyle.

She was given some of my books and tapes, but for months she was afraid to read them and listen to them. Through loving persuasion, she reached out for help, and she was taken through the Steps to Freedom.

The changes in her life are beautiful. The rebellious spirit is gone, and she said, "I feel like I'm in love." And she is in love...with Jesus the lover of her soul. Before, she tried to "make things happen" by attempting to control people or situations in the hope that her needs would be met. But she gave up her struggle for self-fulfillment, and now the Lord is filling her with a growing sense of peace and security. She said, "I no longer want the things I used to crave for; I just want to know Jesus better."

When we attempt to take things into our own hands, we have the feeling of being in control. But what or who are we really controlling? Did we have control of when we were born? To whom we were born? Where we were born? When we will die? Do we have the right or ability to control other people and the circumstances of life so that everything becomes beneficial to ourselves? No, the only real control we have is deciding whom we will serve. Paradoxically, only when we surrender completely to God do we have self-control.[90]

## LIVING UNDER AUTHORITY

The Lord said, "Rebellion is as the sin of divination [witchcraft], and insubordination is as iniquity and idolatry."[91] Defiance against authority places us in the camp of the enemy and subject to his influences. The god of this world, the prince of power of the air, is roaring around like a hungry lion seeking someone to devour. God says, "Get in ranks and follow Me. You are under My protection if you are under My authority." Satan was the originator of rebellion, so when we rebel, we are following his lead. If people truly understood the reality of the spiritual world and the choice they are making, they would immediately renounce any rebellion and submit to God.

We live in a rebellious age. Everyone sits in judgment of those who are in positions of authority over them. We go to church and critique the choir or the music instead of entering into the experience of worshiping God. We sit in judgment of the sermon instead of letting the sermon sit in judgment of us. How many times have you heard people coming out of church criticizing the music or the message? We are critical of our president, our governors, our pastors, our teachers, our spouses, and our parents.

We are commanded by God to submit to and pray for those who are in authority over us. The Apostle Paul wrote, "Let every person be in subjection to the governing authorities. For there is no authority except from God, and those which exist are established by God. Therefore he who resists authority has opposed the ordinance of God; and they who have opposed will receive condemnation upon themselves."[92] God's desire is that we yield ourselves to Him and demonstrate this allegiance by being submissive to those He placed in authority over us. We surrender our right to rule and trust God to work through His established lines of authority for our good. It is a great act of faith to trust God to work through less than perfect people. Actually you are submitting to their position of authority, not the person.

Scripture does teach that there are times when we must obey God rather than man. When governing authorities require us to do something that God commands us not to do, or try to prevent us from doing something that God requires us to do, then we must obey God rather than man, as did the members of the Early Church in special occasions.[93] We also have no obligation to obey people who try to exercise authority outside their jurisdictions. Your employer or school teacher has no right to tell you what to do in your own home. A policeman cannot tell you what to believe or where to go to church, but he can tell you to pull your car over and give you a ticket if you are breaking the law.

## RELATING TO AUTHORITY

Daniel is a powerful example of submission. It could be argued that King Nebuchadnezzar overstepped his authority by requiring Daniel and his people to do something that went against their faith. Notice how Daniel responded. He showed respect to the king and those who carried out the king's commands. Nebuchadnezzar wanted those who were in his service to eat the food he chose.

Daniel did not want to defile himself with the king's food, so he sought permission from his immediate superior to eat as God required, as long as he remained healthy enough to be a servant of the King, which is all the King really wanted. Because he was not defiant, nor disrespectful, "God granted Daniel favor and compassion in the sight of the commander of the officials."[94] Daniel offered a creative alternative that allowed the commander to save face in the sight of the king and to also fulfill the wishes of the king to have wise and healthy servants.

The Lord's Prayer[95] is a model for how we are to appeal to those who are in authority over us. First, we must have a right standing, which is reflected in the phrase, "Our Father who art in heaven, hallowed be Thy name." In most judicial systems, we must approach the judge in a court of law with respect. It would be considered contempt of court if we didn't. We respectfully address the judge as "Your honor."

If there are any unresolved personal issues between yourself and the one you wish to make an appeal to, you better get them resolved first. That is true for our God as well as judges in courts of law or supervisors at work. We couldn't approach God until He found a way to forgive us, and any judge who is personally biased toward or against the accused must remove himself from the case. If a teenager has been disrespectful and disobedient to his father, he should get that straightened out before he asks for the keys to the car.

Second, we should be committed to the success of those who are in authority and willing to do their will as long as it doesn't violate who we are in Christ. This principle is reflected in the phrase, "Thy kingdom come. Thy will be done, on earth as it is in heaven" (v. 10). We must do nothing that would hinder them from carrying out their God-given responsibilities. People in leadership cannot accomplish much without the loyal support of those who are under them. Those who are in a submissive role will not prosper in their rebellion. Scripture says, "Obey your leaders, and submit to them; for they keep watch over your souls, as those who will give an account. Let them do this with joy and not with grief, for this would be unprofitable for you."[96]

One of Satan's more potent strategies is to discredit spiritual leaders. Your loyalty to those who are in authority over you will be tested. This fact is especially true in Christian ministries and in the home. Everybody will be tempted with subtle thoughts such as: I don't like the way he did that; I could do it better than that; This is what I would do if I were in that position; or I'm the one who should be running the show around here. It doesn't make any difference if those thoughts come from the pit, from other disloyal members or from your own flesh; they are wrong according to James 3:13-18:

Who among you is wise and understanding?
Let him show by his good behavior his deeds in
the gentleness of wisdom. But if you have bitter

jealousy and selfish ambition in your heart, do
not be arrogant and so lie against the truth.
This wisdom is not that which comes down from
above, but is earthly, natural, demonic. For where
jealousy and selfish ambition exist, there is disorder
and every evil thing. But the wisdom from above is
first pure, then peaceable, gentle, reasonable, full
of mercy and good fruits, unwavering, without
hypocrisy. And the seed whose fruit is righteousness
is sown in peace by those who make peace.

Most leaders will listen to our appeals if they know we
are concerned for their responsibilities and their reputa-
tions. The Lord withheld judgment upon the Israelites
when Moses petitioned Him. He based his appeal on the
reputation of God.[97] God can only bless us if we are submissive,[98] and in doing so, we find favor with Him.[99] Life
will be more difficult for us if the ones we are serving are
failing in their responsibilities. Every passage that commands us to be submissive ends in a promise for the ones
who are—and condemnation for those who aren't.

Third, our appeals must be based on legitimate needs.
This principle is reflected in the phrase, "Give us this day
our daily bread."[100] Every leader is subject to the needs of
those he serves, and the Lord will bring conviction upon
those who do not hear the legitimate cries of their people.
However, requests for selfish desires may justifiably go
unanswered. Few things can turn off a parent more than an
ungrateful child who demands more than what is needed.

Fourth, our appeals must come from hearts that are free from bitterness. This principle is reflected in the phrase, "And forgive us our debts, as we also have forgiven our debtors."[101] Anyone who has allowed a root of bitterness to spring up and defile others should not expect favor from those who are in authority. When Simon requested authority from the apostles, Peter refused saying, "You are in the gall of bitterness and in the bondage of iniquity."[102]

Fifth, our appeals should be for proper direction in life, which is reflected in the phrase, "And do not lead us into temptation, but deliver us from evil."[103] Every human institution has been given its authority by God "for the punishment of evildoers and the praise of those who do right."[104]

## TRUST GOD'S PROTECTION

Daniel also taught us to trust in God's protection and provision when we cannot in good conscience do what the king commands. King Darius was persuaded to "establish a statute and enforce an injunction that anyone who makes a petition to any god or man besides you, O king, for thirty days, shall be cast into the lions' den."[105] Daniel could not honor that decree, and so he continued to pray and give thanks to almighty God. He ended up in the lions' den, and the Lord shut the mouths of the lions.

If your boss wants you to lie, don't be disrespectful. Appeal to him or her as outlined above and offer an alternative. What if the boss won't accept your alternative and says, "If you won't do what I tell you to do, then I will get someone in here who will?" Then let him or her get someone who will, and trust God to provide for your needs.

## DEAL WITH ABUSE

What if the authority figure is abusive? Is it being rebellious to turn him in? Absolutely not! It is wrong for Christian leaders to tell battered wives and abused children to go home and be submissive. "But that is what Scripture requires," says the abuser. That is not all Scripture says on the issue. God has established governing institutions to protect battered wives and abused children. The heart of God goes out to the weak and the defenseless. "This is pure and undefiled religion in the sight of our God and Father, to visit orphans and widows in their distress."[106]

Turn the abusers in to the authorities whom God has established. This action is not being vindictive for two reasons. First, abusive leaders have obviously abdicated their responsibility to provide for and protect those whom they were charged by God to watch over. Being abused by the one in authority over you doubles the offense. Not only are you being abused, but you have also lost your God-intended protection.

Second, you will never help abusers by allowing them to continue in their abuses. They are hurting people who need help. If they aren't stopped, the cycle of abuse will just continue on. Stopping them actually demonstrates care for the abusers. They have a right to find their forgiveness and freedom in Christ like anybody else, but many won't take that opportunity if they are allowed to continue in sin. If you were abused by your father, and your mother knew about it, but wouldn't do anything to help you, who would be harder to forgive? Everybody knows it would be the mother.

I am not saying that we don't have to be submissive to people in positions of authority simply because they are not perfect. If that were the case, nobody would be submissive to anyone but God. What I am saying is that there is a biblical means by which we can appeal to those less-than-perfect people who are in authority, and there are times when we must obey God rather than man. Determining when to reject man's authority requires discernment and a deep inner conviction based on truth that cannot be compromised regardless of the consequences. You are acting rebelliously if you refuse to submit simply because you would prefer to do it your way.

## THE MEANING OF SUBMISSION

Because of abusive authority and legalistic teaching, the term submission has a negative connotation for many people. To them, a submissive person is a doormat who never questions those in authority. Some accept the doormat role and identity, while others deeply resent all authority figures, including God. But God is not like the abusive authority figures they have known. He has our best interests at heart. Submitting to His will and His way is the only means by which we can have any sense of social order. Little would be accomplished in our marriages, families, churches, businesses, and governments without some authoritative structure. When none exists, there can only be anarchy. The authority of God provides for the peaceful coexistence of His people, who are called to live and work together.

The Apostle Paul instructs wives to be submissive to their husbands, and then he says that we are all (both men and women) to "be subject to one another in the fear of Christ."[107] This means that all Christians are to be willing to cooperate in their relationships under God-given authority structures. Everybody is under the authority of somebody or something, and we are all subject to the needs of one another, because we are all called to love one another.

## SUBMISSION, REBELLION, AND THE SEARCH FOR SIGNIFICANCE

What do Paul and Peter mean when they teach that wives are to be submissive to their husbands?[108] Why do some women rebel against the idea of submission? Why do some men abuse the authority God has given them in the home? Why do Peter and Paul remind men of their responsibility to lovingly meet the needs of their wives?[109]

These are critical questions that we all encounter when treading into the minefield of role relationships in marriage. Much of the confusion and virtually all of the emotional energy that fuels the debate comes from buying into a wrong view of the source of our identities and significance. People tend to get their identities from the things they do and their significance from their positions and

> It is not what we do that determines who we are; it is who we are that determines what we do.

titles. They wrongly conclude appearance, performance, and status equals significance.

Our identities are not determined by what we do; they are determined by who we are in Christ. It is not what we do that determines who we are; it is who we are that determines what we do. Before coming to Christ, we did get our identities from our natural heritage, professional work, and social status. But now that we are in Christ, "There is neither Greek and Jew, circumcised and uncircumcised, barbarian and Scythian, slave and freeman, but Christ is all, and in all,"[110] and "neither male nor female."[111] These passages do not eradicate social roles or eliminate authoritative structure. It clearly teaches that our essential identities are found in Christ, and we are to live out our roles in life as children of God.

Our significance is not determined by our worldly positions and possessions, but by our position in Christ and the riches we possess in Him. When the mother of the sons of Zebedee was trying to get her sons seated next to Christ, our Lord used the occasion to instruct us concerning positions of ministry. "You know that the rulers of the Gentiles lord it over them, and their great men exercise authority over them. It is not so among you, but whoever wishes to become great among you shall be your servant, and whoever wishes to be first among you shall be your slave."[112] Every leader is subject to the needs of those who serve under him. Headship in the home is not a right to be demanded; it is an awesome responsibility, and the same holds for any role of social responsibility.

## IDENTITY DETERMINES SIGNIFICANCE

The world says you are nothing; therefore, you better scheme, achieve, and get ahead, which leads to malice, guile, hypocrisy, envy, and slander.[113] The Bible tells us that we are something; therefore, we should be submissive.[114] The scriptural commands concerning roles in relationships are given in a context where the significance question has already been settled by our identities and positions in Christ.

> But you are a chosen race, a royal priesthood, a holy
> nation, a people for God's own possession, that you
> may proclaim the excellencies of Him who has called
> you out of darkness into His marvelous light; for
> you once were not a people, but now you are the
> people of God; you had not received mercy, but now
> you have received mercy.[115]

The biblical formula reads: our position in Christ and our identities as children of God equals significance. If a wife's sense of significance flows from her relationship with God, she can respond to her husband's leadership because in fact she is equally significant in God's plan for her personally, her marriage, and her family. Husbands don't need to demand respect or lord it over others to have any sense of worth. They already are significant as a children of God and secure in Christ. They are free to be the true servant-leader God has called them to be. The fruit of the Spirit is not staff control, nor spouse control, nor child control; it is self-control. Both the husband and wife can respond with grace to a less-than-perfect spouse, because they don't need the other person to meet their need for significance.[116]

Submission, authority, and control concern not only man/wife issues, or parent/child issues, or employer/employee issues. Submission is primarily a relational matter between the creature and the Creator. When we know who we are as children of God, we don't have to rebel, we don't have to dominate and control. We yield to the Lordship of Christ, secure in our position in Him, and relate to others with love and forgiveness.

## STEP FOUR: DEALING WITH REBELLION

The Apostle James wrote, "Submit therefore to God. Resist the devil and he will flee from you."[117] Submitting to God enables us to resist the devil. The prayer that begins this Step is a commitment to forsake rebellion and choose a submissive spirit, as follows:

> **Dear Heavenly Father,** *You have said in the Bible that rebellion is the same thing as witchcraft and as bad as idolatry* (see 1 Samuel 15:23). *I know I have not always been submissive, but instead I have rebelled in my heart against You and against those You have placed in authority over me. I pray that You would show me all the ways I have been rebellious. I choose to adopt a submissive spirit and a servant's heart. In Jesus' precious name I pray.* **Amen.**

## AREAS OF REBELLION

As the Lord leads you, prayerfully consider the ways you have been rebellious toward the following lines of authority:

- ▲ Civil government including traffic laws, tax laws, attitude toward government officials (See Romans 13:1-7; 1 Timothy 2:1-4; 1 Peter 2:13-17.)
- ▲ Parents, stepparents, or legal guardians (See Ephesians 6:1-3.)
- ▲ Teachers, coaches, school officials (See Romans 13:1-4.)
- ▲ Employers (past and present) (See 1 Peter 2:18-23.)

▲ Husband (See 1 Peter 3:1-4.) or Wife
(See Ephesians 5:21; 1 Peter 3:7.)
{Note to husbands: Take a moment and ask
the Lord if your lack of love for your wife could
be fostering a rebellious spirit within her.
If so, confess that now as a violation of
Ephesians 5:22, 23.}

▲ Church leaders (See Hebrews 13:17.)

▲ God (See Daniel 9:5, 9.)

The following prayer is an opportunity for you to confess
your rebellion:

**Lord Jesus,** *I confess that I have been rebellious*
*toward* _____ (name or position), *by*
(specially confess what you did or did not do).
*Thank You for Your forgiveness. I choose to be*
*submissive and obedient to Your Word. In Jesus'*
*name I pray.* **Amen.**

# Chapter Six
## OVERCOMING PRIDE

In the northern reaches of Canada, the story is told of two geese and a turtle that developed a deep friendship. As the nights became shorter and cooler, the geese started talking about flying south for the winter. One evening as the three animals huddled together, the geese wondered openly about their friend the turtle.

"We're sure going to miss you," said one goose. "Since you can't walk south for the winter, what are you going to do?"

"I have an idea," said the turtle. "Why don't we find a sturdy stick that the two of you can hold in your mouths. I will hold on to the stick in the middle with my powerful teeth. Then when you fly south for the winter, I will fly with you."

"Do you think you are strong enough to hold on for that long?" asked the other goose.

"Sure, I'm very strong," said the turtle.

Several weeks later, somewhere over Montana, a farmer looked up and saw the most incredible thing he had ever seen. He rushed into the house to tell his wife. When she ran outside and saw two geese flying overhead with a stick in their mouths and a turtle hanging between them, she cried out, "What an incredible idea! Who thought of that?"

Knowing it was his idea, the turtle couldn't resist saying, "I did!" And down went the turtle.

## THE UGLY FIVE-LETTER WORD

Pride is a killer. It comes before a fall. Pride is a five-letter word with I in the middle. Pride says, "It was my idea, and I can do it by my strength and resources." Pride is the origin of evil. Scripture says of Satan, "But you said in your heart, 'I will ascend to heaven; I will raise my throne above the stars of God, and I will sit on the mount of assembly in the recesses of the north. I will ascend above the heights of the clouds; I will make myself like the Most High.' Nevertheless you will be thrust down to Sheol, to the recesses of the pit."[118] Hell is where we say, "My will be done." Heaven is where we say, "Thy will be done."

> Pride is a five-letter word with I in the middle.

Notice the connection between pride and spiritual warfare in the following two passages:

> But He gives a greater grace. Therefore it says, "God is opposed to the proud, but gives grace to the humble." Submit therefore to God. Resist the devil and he will flee from you (James 4:6, 7).

> All of you clothe yourselves with humility toward one another, for God is opposed to the proud, but gives grace to the humble. Humble yourselves, therefore, under the mighty hand of God, that He may exalt you at the proper time, casting all your anxiety upon Him, because He cares for you. Be of sober spirit, be on the alert. Your adversary, the devil, prowls about like a roaring lion, seeking someone to devour. But resist him (1 Peter 5:5-9).

## SELF-SUFFICIENCY HAS A PRICE

After Jesus fed the 5,000, He sent the disciples across the Sea of Galilee while He went up to the mountain to pray. In the middle of the sea, the disciples encountered a storm: "And seeing them straining at the oars...He came to them, walking on the sea; and He intended to pass by them."[119] The Lord intends to pass by the self-sufficient. Go ahead and row against the storms of life. He will let you until your arms fall off, but those who call upon the name of the Lord will be saved.

The only answer the world has for those who are caught in the storms of life is "Row harder, or give in to the pressure and learn to live at sea!" The devil says, "You can do it by yourself, but if you need a little extra power, I can arrange that for a small price." Pride says, "I think I can get out of this by myself. All it requires is a lot of hard work, human ingenuity, and maybe a little luck." God says, "I won't interfere with your plans. If you want to try to save yourself, solve your own problems or meet your own needs, you have My permission. But you won't be able to, because in the final analysis, you absolutely need Me, and you necessarily need each other." Fallen humanity is on a sinking ship that is going nowhere without God.

Pride can sneak up on the best of us. King Uzziah was a godly man who reigned for 52 years,[120] and "he did right in the sight of the Lord." His accomplishments were exceptional. He built a strong army and fortified the city. "Hence his fame spread afar, for he was marvelously helped until he was strong. But when he became strong, his heart was so proud that he acted corruptly, and he was unfaithful to the Lord his God."

The more we are able to accomplish, the more susceptible we are to pride. More than one Christian leader has fallen when he started receiving glowing accolades for his work. "Therefore let him who thinks he stands take heed lest he fall."[121]

# FALSE AND TRUE HUMILITY

What is humility? Is it groveling around in poverty, proclaiming our worthless state? No, that is counterfeit humility that leads only to defeat. Paul says, "Let no one keep defrauding you of your prize by delighting in self-abasement."[122]

Humility is not saying God is everything and we are nothing. That is a form of false humility. Christ didn't die on the cross for nothing. He was crucified to redeem a fallen humanity. Throughout the New Testament, we are admonished to build up one another, and we are strongly warned against any attempt to tear down one another, including ourselves.

Paul tells us, "For through the grace given to me I say to every man among you not to think more highly of himself than he ought to think; but to think so as to have sound judgment, as God has allotted to each a measure of faith."[123] That is not a call for self-abasement; it is a call for sound judgment. Paul says of himself, "By the grace of God I am what I am, and His grace toward me did not prove vain; but I labored even more than all of them, yet not I, but the grace of God with me."[124]

> Humility is confidence properly placed.

We are what we are by the grace of God! To deny that would be to discredit the work that Christ accomplished on the cross. To believe that we are more than we are, or to believe that we are products of our own doing, is to join the ranks of the deceived millions who have fallen victim to pride.

Humility is confidence properly placed. So Paul says, "Put no confidence in the flesh."[125] But we ought to have all the confidence that our faith can muster in God and in what He can do through us. We should all want ourselves and all the children of God to reach their highest potential in Christ. "By this is my Father glorified, that you bear much fruit, and so prove to be my disciples."[126] Pride says, "I did it." True humility says, "I did it by the grace of God."

Cowering in some corner in unbelief or groveling around in mock humility in utter defeat brings no glory to God. "Let your light shine before men in such a way that they may see your good works, and glorify your Father who is in heaven."[127]

The glory of God is a manifestation of His presence. When we glorify God in our bodies, we manifest His presence in the world. The only way we can glorify God in our bodies is to live victorious lives and bear much fruit. And the only way we can live victorious lives and bear much fruit is to abide in Christ.[128] That is why we must come to terms with our pride—so we can be established in Christ, "in whom we have boldness and confident access through faith in Him."[129]

## AVENUES OF PRIDE

People come from diverse backgrounds, but pride, rebellion, and self-sufficiency are consequences of the Fall and common to all humanity. The whole aim of Satan is to get self-interest recognized as the chief end of man. Satan is called the "prince of this world" because self-interest rules this world. The iniquity that is passed on from one generation to another is a distortion of, and preoccupation with, self-will. This self-will is the chief characteristic of the false prophet and teacher. Peter says they "indulge the flesh in its corrupt desires and despise authority. Daring, self-willed, they do not tremble when they revile angelic majesties."[130] They operate from independent spirits and won't answer to anyone. An even more sober scenario is given in Matthew 7:20-23:

> So then, you will know them by their fruits. Not everyone who says to Me, "Lord, Lord," will enter the kingdom of heaven; but he who does the will of My Father who is in heaven. Many will say to Me on that day, "Lord, Lord, did we not prophesy in Your name, and in Your name cast out demons, and in Your name perform many miracles?" And then I will declare to them, "I never knew you; depart from Me, you who practice lawlessness [iniquity]."

Strongholds of pride are not only passed on from one generation to the next, but each new generation will develop its own basis for pride by seeking fame and fortune in the worldly system in which it is raised. Self-glorification can come by accumulating wealth, garnering social status, acquiring academic degrees, and even obtaining biblical knowledge. There is nothing wrong with having wealth, social status, academic degrees, or biblical knowledge—if they are obtained by the grace of God for the purpose of doing His will.

Pride is the chief characteristic of the world: "For everything in the world—the cravings of sinful man, the lust of his eyes and the boasting of what he has and does—comes not from the Father but from the world."[131] All temptation is an attempt to get us to live our lives independently of God. When we give into such temptation, we unwittingly serve the world, the flesh, or the devil. We have been deceived into thinking we are benefiting ourselves, but such temporal gratification quickly fades away. Jesus counters by sharing the way of the Cross, the foundational principle for our lives in Christ, which is the repudiation of the old natural life and embracing the new joyful union with the resurrected life of Christ.

Though the immediate evidence of pride is self-centeredness, the root of pride is self-exaltation. It is at this point that we are most like the evil "god of this world." Self-exaltation expressed by subtle attitudes of pride and self-righteousness will keep a person from humbly admitting the need for Christ's righteousness. Such pride is an open invitation to the god of this world, which may render impossible the ability to carry out even the best of our intentions. Notice how this proved to be true in the life of Peter.

Jesus said to Peter, "Simon, Simon, behold, Satan has demanded permission to sift you like wheat; but I have prayed for you, that your faith may not fail; and you, when once you have turned again, strengthen your brothers."[132] Notice that Jesus didn't say He would not permit Satan to sift Peter like wheat. He just said He would pray for him, that he would be able to help others if he repented.

What right did Satan have to ask permission of God? The previous context reveals that a dispute had arisen among the apostles regarding who was the greatest. Such pride can coexist with the best of intentions. Peter said, "Lord, with You I am ready to go both to prison and to death." Sadly, he had already forfeited his right. Before the cock crowed, Peter denied his Lord three times.

## A BIBLICAL VIEW OF OUR WORTH

A proper sense of worth comes from recognizing and appropriating the biblical fact that we are loved and valued by our heavenly Father. Our value is not based on our own merit but on the fact that we are His precious children for whom Christ was willing to die. We are blessed with every spiritual blessing...chosen in God...holy and blameless before Him...predestined to adoption as sons...have redemption and forgiveness...the riches of His grace are lavished on us.[133]

The problem is not that we don't have tremendous riches in Christ; the problem is we don't see them. So Paul wrote, "I pray that the eyes of your heart may be enlightened, so that you may know what is the hope of His calling, what are the riches of the glory of His inheritance in the saints ."[134]

## Going Through Step Five

"God is opposed to the proud, but gives grace to the humble."[135] By acknowledging pride, we are declaring what Satan refused to declare—that we are dependent upon God. By exposing and confessing pride, we are acknowledging our desire to be free from a self-centered and a self-sufficient life. Then we will be free to begin living by the grace of God and deriving our spiritual strengths and identities from God, through Christ. Ask God to guide you with the following prayer:

*Dear Heavenly Father, You have said that pride goes before destruction and an arrogant spirit before stumbling. I confess that I have focused on my own needs and desires and not others. I have not always denied myself, picked up my cross daily and followed You. I have relied on my own strength and resources instead of resting in Yours. I have placed my will before Yours and centered my life around myself instead of You. I confess my pride and selfishness and pray that all ground gained in my life by the*

*enemies of the Lord Jesus Christ would be canceled.*
*I choose to rely upon the Holy Spirit's power and*
*guidance so that I will do nothing from selfishness or*
*empty conceit. With humility of mind, I choose to*
*regard others as more important than myself. I*
*acknowledge You as my Lord and confess that apart*
*from You I can do nothing of lasting significance.*
*Please examine my heart and show me the specific*
*ways I have lived my life in pride. In the gentle and*
*humble name of Jesus I pray. **Amen.***
(See Proverbs 16:18; Matthew 6:33; 16:24;
Romans 12:10; Philippians. 2:3.)

Pray through the list below and use the prayer following
to confess any sins of pride the Lord brings to mind.

- ❏ Having a stronger desire to do my will
  than God's will
- ❏ Leaning too much on my own understanding
  and experience rather than seeking God's
  guidance through prayer and His Word
- ❏ Relying on my own strengths and resources
  instead of depending on the power of the
  Holy Spirit
- ❏ Being more concerned about controlling others
  than in developing self-control
- ❏ Being too busy doing "important" and selfish
  things rather than seeking and doing God's will
- ❏ Having a tendency to think that I have no needs

❏ Finding it hard to admit when I am wrong

❏ Being more concerned about pleasing people than pleasing God

❏ Being overly concerned about getting the credit I feel I deserve

❏ Thinking I am more humble, spiritual, religious, or devoted than others

❏ Being driven to obtain recognition by attaining degrees, titles, and positions

❏ Often feeling that my needs are more important than another person's needs

❏ Considering myself better than others because of my academic, artistic, athletic abilities, and accomplishments

❏ Having feelings of inferiority appearing as false humility

❏ Not waiting on God

❏ Other ways I have thought more highly of myself than I should

For each of the above areas that has been true in your life, pray aloud:

***Lord Jesus,*** *I agree I have been proud by* (name what you checked above). *Thank You for Your forgiveness. I choose to humble myself before You and others. I choose to place all my confidence in You and put not confidence in my flesh. In Jesus' name I pray.* ***Amen.***

## HEALING FOLLOWS HUMILITY

The following letter was received from a pastor who was caught in a sexual addiction and powerfully illustrates that God is opposed to the proud, but gives grace to the humble:

> Realizing that I needed to be accountable to someone and to bring these urges to light, so as to break their power over me, I shared these feelings with my wife and the men in my Bible study group, so they could pray for me and hold me accountable.
>
> They were all very supportive, though a little shaken that someone in ministry would share such a personal matter with them. I expressed that I am only a brother in Christ and not superior to them in any way, and that if we were ever to be of one mind and one accord, we would need to be open with one another.
>
> I must admit that it was easy to be open, because *I know who I am in Christ.* I believe that this temptation will soon be a thing of the past. My past no longer has a hold on me. I am accountable to others, and I have prayer partners. Victory is mine!

# Chapter Seven
## OVERCOMING HABITUAL SIN

Suppose you could see the reality of the spiritual world as God does and knew what people were thinking. You observed a dark brooding angelic figure lurking outside the door of a young Christian named Danny.

Disguised as an angel of light, this demon subtly suggests that Danny open the door to sin: *Why don't you take a peek at that pornography? You know you want to. You will get away with it. Who would know? Everybody else does it.*

The Holy Spirit within Danny brings immediate conviction and offers a way of escape. Danny also has a physical appetite for food and sex, as well as old flesh patterns that operate independently of God. The old nature wants to be satisfied and argues against the Spirit of God: *What's wrong with looking at pornography anyway? After all, who created me to have all these desires? Wasn't it God? How could He create me a certain way and then condemn me for it?*

The battle in the mind is intense, "For the flesh sets its desire against the Spirit, and the Spirit against the flesh; for these are in opposition to one another."[136] God offered Danny a way of escape, but he failed to take every thought captive to the obedience of Christ.[137] At first the pictures are a delight to the eyes, and the body responds with a euphoric explosion of feelings. But the pleasure is only for a moment, because "each one is tempted when he is carried away and enticed by his own lust. Then when lust has conceived, it gives birth to sin; and when sin is accomplished, it brings forth death."[138]

## CONSEQUENCES TO WRONG CHOICES

The brooding figure takes advantage of the open door, because Danny acted independently of God by choosing to sin. Satan's role as the tempter changes immediately to the role of the accuser: "You will never get away with this. How can you call yourself a Christian and do what you do? You're pathetic!"

Overcome by guilt, Danny cries out to God, "Lord, forgive me; I'll never do it again." Two days later, Danny sins again, which precipitates another cry for forgiveness. As the downward spiral of sin, confess, sin, confess, and sin again continues, another event takes place.

Danny is caught in his sin by another "Christian," who knows nothing of compassion.

Instead of responding as a minister of grace and reconciliation, he joins with the brooding figure in a "ministry" of condemnation.

"You're a pathetic example of what a real Christian is supposed to be!" he says to Danny. "How can you do that and call yourself a Christian? You're an embarrassment to the Church. You better confess it and beg God's forgiveness." Legalistic controlling "Christians" are in league with the accuser of the brethren, and they don't even know it.

This "Christian" accuser doesn't seem to know that Danny is already forgiven by God and that he has probably confessed his sin a hundred times before. His merciless and insensitive response will only drive Danny to greater depths of despair. Adding guilt and shame does not enhance mental health. The world, the flesh, and the devil have brought another saint to his knees. How does one break this cycle of defeat? Is confession enough?

> Complete repentance means to submit to God, resist the devil, and close the door to future temptations.

To confess means to agree with God or to walk in the light as He is in the light.[139] It is the critical first step in repentance, but it is not complete repentance and won't be until there is a demonstrated change. We must agree with God and face the truth, but that alone will not deal with sin's entrapment. You have submitted to God, if the confession was genuine and accompanied by a commitment to do His will, but you haven't yet resisted the devil.[140]

Complete repentance means to submit to God, resist the devil, and close the door to future temptations. That means getting rid of the pornography in your home, and on your computer. It means staying away from bars, drug dealers, and inappropriate relationships. It means that you "abstain from every form of evil."[141] It may mean that you change your phone number, so drug dealers and other undesirables can't contact you. The door will be completely closed when all the bondages have been broken and all the mental strongholds have been torn down. The latter includes renouncing the lies you have believed that contributed to the sinful behavior, and then choosing the truth. This Step is intended to break the bondages and tear down the mental strongholds. You will be transformed when you renew your mind to the truth of God's Word.[142]

## THE EFFECTS OF ADDICTION

People caught in addictive and immoral patterns of behavior are subjected to some of the cruelest harassment of the enemy. First, Satan tempts them to sin, then he mercilessly condemns them for sinning, and then he attacks their sense of worth. If they believe the lies they will start thinking that they are nothing more than a hopeless sinner, alcoholic, or addict.

You do not have a chemical problem, or sex problem, or drug problem, you have a life problem. You will not be successful just trying to eliminate bad behavior; telling you that what you are doing is wrong does not give you the power to stop doing it. You need to get right with God, and then the life of Christ will be manifested in you, and you will have the power of God to overcome the sin. If you are filled (controlled) by the Holy Spirit, you will not carry out the desires of the flesh.[143] You don't need condemnation! You want to be free from sin, because nobody likes to live in bondage to sin.

## GOING THROUGH STEP SIX

Overcoming habitual sin may require help from a trusted brother or sister in Christ. James 5:16 says, "Confess your sins to one another, and pray for one another, so that you may be healed. The effective prayer of a righteous man can accomplish much." Sometimes the assurance of 1 John 1:9 is enough: "If we confess our sins, He is faithful and righteous to forgive us our sins and to cleanse us from all unrighteousness."

Confession is not saying, I'm sorry. It is openly admitting, I did it. Whether you need help from other people or just the accountability of walking in the light before God, pray the following prayer aloud:

*Dear Heavenly Father,* You have told me to put on the Lord Jesus Christ and make no provision for the flesh in regard to its lust. I confess that I have given in to fleshly lusts that wage war against my soul. I thank You that in Christ my sins are already forgiven, but I have broken Your holy law and I have allowed sin to wage war in my body. I come to You now to confess and renounce these sins of the flesh so that I might be cleansed and set free from the bondage of sin. Please reveal to my mind all the sins of the flesh I have committed and the ways I have grieved the Holy Spirit. In Jesus' holy name, I pray. **Amen.**[144]

The following list contains many sins of the flesh, but a prayerful examination of Mark 7:20-23, Galatians 5:19-21, Ephesians 4:25-31, and other Scripture passages will help you to be even more thorough. Look over the list below and the Scriptures just listed and ask the Holy Spirit to bring to your mind the ones you need to confess. He may reveal others to you as well. For each one the Lord shows you, pray a prayer of confession from your heart. There is a sample prayer following the list. (Note: Sexual sins, eating disorders, substance abuse, abortion, suicidal tendencies, and perfectionism will be dealt with later in this step.)

❏ Stealing          ❏ Quarreling/Fighting
❏ Jealousy/Envy     ❏ Complaining/Criticism
❏ Sarcasm           ❏ Lustful Actions

- ☐ Gossip/Slander
- ☐ Apathy/Laziness
- ☐ Hatred
- ☐ Lustful Thoughts
- ☐ Cheating
- ☐ Greed/Materialism
- ☐ Swearing
- ☐ Lying
- ☐ Anger
- ☐ Drunkenness
- ☐ Procrastination
- ☐ Others

For each item that you checked above, confess to the Lord as follows:

> **Lord Jesus,** *I confess that I have sinned against You by* (name the sins). *Thank You for Your forgiveness and cleansing. I now turn away from these expressions of sin and turn to You, Lord. Fill me with Your Holy Spirit so that I will not carry out the desires of the flesh. In Jesus' name I pray.* **Amen.**

Note: If you are struggling with habitual sin, read *Overcoming Addictive Behavior* (Regal Books, 2003).

## UNDERSTANDING SEXUAL BONDAGES

The Apostle Paul identifies every child of God with Christ in His life, death, burial, and resurrection in Romans 6. That association is true, because our souls are in union with God, and His life is eternal. We are to continuously choose to believe that we are alive in Christ and dead to sin. There is a law of sin and a law of death and laws cannot be done away with. But they can be overcome by a greater law, which is the law of life in Christ Jesus.[145]

So sin is still present and tempting, and physical death is still imminent. But the law of life in Christ Jesus ensures us that we will continue to live spiritually and be forever in the presence of God. And the law of life in Christ Jesus is greater than the law of sin. As long as we live by faith according to

> We are to continuously choose to believe that we are alive in Christ and dead to sin.

what God says is true and in His power, we will not sin. Paul goes on to say that it is our responsibility not to let sin reign in our mortal body, and he tells us how. "Do not go on presenting the members of your body to sin as instruments of unrighteousness; but present yourselves to God as those alive from the dead, and your members as instruments of righteousness to God."[146]

If you commit a sexual sin you use your body as an instrument of unrighteousness and you allow sin to reign in your mortal body. Confession alone will not resolve this. There is one other passage in the Bible that is important for overcoming sexual strongholds as follows:

> Do you not know that your bodies are members of Christ? Shall I then take away the members of Christ and make them members of a harlot? May it never be! Or do you not know that the one who joins himself to a harlot is one body with her? For He says,

"The two will become one flesh." But the one who joins himself to the Lord is one spirit with Him. Flee immorality. Every other sin that a man commits is outside the body, but the immoral man sins against his own body. Or do you not know that your body is a temple of the Holy Spirit who is in you, whom you have from God, and that you are not your own? For you have been bought with a price: therefore glorify God in your body (1 Corinthians 6:15-20).

## SEXUAL BONDING

Bonding takes place when unholy sex is committed. The person has become one flesh with his or her partner. That is true even in the case of incest or rape. The body is used as an instrument of unrighteousness. The temple is violated. But that isn't fair! Of course it's not fair, and I can't promise that it won't happen to you or anyone else. But I can tell you how to resolve it in Christ so that you don't have to stay in bondage to the sexual abuse. We have observed that if there is voluntary compliance with the sexual abuser, the victim usually will become very sexually active. In cases of rape and incest, a woman will usually shut down sexually, even if she is now married to a Christian husband. Sex is dirty in her mind, and she can't stand to be touched.

We are warned to flee from any form of immorality, because it is a self-destructive sin that we commit against our own bodies. God and Satan both know our weakness to sexual passions. Satan plays on that weakness, but God provides a way of escape.

## BREAKING SEXUAL BONDING

For complete repentance, ask the Lord to reveal every sexual use of your body as an instrument of unrighteousness. As the Lord brings each one to mind, renounce every sexual use of your body as an instrument of unrighteousness and ask God to break the bond with that person. Then conclude by presenting your body to the Lord as a living sacrifice. We are urged by the mercies of God to do that.[147] Start by asking the Lord to guide you as follows:

> **Lord Jesus,** *I have allowed sin to reign in my mortal body. I ask You to bring to my mind every sexual use of my body as an instrument of unrighteousness so that I can renounce these sexual sins and break those sinful bondages. In Jesus' name I pray.* **Amen.**

As the Lord brings to your mind every immoral sexual use of your body, whether it was done to you (rape, incest, sexual molestation) or willingly by you (pornography, masturbation, sexual immorality), renounce every experience as follows:

*Lord Jesus, I renounce* (name the sexual experience) *with* (name). *I ask You to break that sinful bond with* (name) *spiritually, physically and emotionally.* **Amen.**

After you are finished, commit your body to the Lord by praying:

*Lord Jesus, I renounce all these uses of my body as an instrument of unrighteousness, and I admit to any willful participation. I choose to present my physical body to You as an instrument of righteousness, a living and holy sacrifice, acceptable to You. I choose to reserve the sexual use of my body for marriage only. I reject the devil's lie that my body is not clean or that it is dirty or in any way unacceptable to You as a result of my past sexual experiences. Lord, thank You that You have cleansed and forgiven me and that You love and accept me just the way I am. Therefore, I choose now to accept myself and my body as clean in Your eyes. In Jesus' name I pray.* **Amen.**

# PRAYERS FOR SPECIFIC PROBLEMS

## Pornography

*Lord Jesus, I confess that I have looked at sexually suggestive and pornographic material for the purpose of stimulating myself sexually. I have attempted to satisfy my lustful desires and polluted my body, soul, and spirit. Thank You for cleansing me and for Your forgiveness. I renounce any satanic bonds I have allowed in my life through the unrighteous use of my body and mind. Lord, I commit myself to destroy any objects in my possession that I have used for sexual stimulation and to turn away from all media that are associated with my sexual sin. I commit myself to the renewing of my mind and to think pure thoughts. Fill me with your Holy Spirit that I may not carry out the desires of the flesh. In Jesus' name I pray.* **Amen.**

## Homosexuality

**Lord Jesus,** *I renounce the lie that You have created me or anyone else to be homosexual and I agree that in Your Word You clearly forbid homosexual behavior. I choose to accept myself as a child of God and I thank You that You created me as a man* (woman). *I renounce all homosexual thoughts, urges, drives, and acts and renounce all ways that Satan has used these things to pervert my relationships. I announce that I am free in Christ to relate to the opposite sex and my own sex in the way that You intended. In Jesus' name I pray.* **Amen.**

## Abortion

**Lord Jesus,** *I confess that I was not a proper guardian and keeper of the life You entrusted to me, and I confess that I have sinned. Thank You that because of Your forgiveness, I can forgive myself. I* *commit the child to You for all eternity and believe that he or she is in Your caring hands. In Jesus' name I pray.* **Amen.**

## Suicidal Tendencies

**Lord Jesus,** *I renounce all suicidal thoughts and any attempts I've made to take my own life or in any way injure myself. I renounce the lie that life is hopeless and that I can find peace and freedom by taking my own life. Satan is a thief and comes to steal, kill, and destroy. I choose life in Christ who said He came to give me life and give it abundantly. Thank You for Your forgiveness that allows me to forgive myself. I choose to believe that there is always hope in Christ and that my heavenly Father love me. In Jesus' name, I pray.* **Amen.**

## Drivenness and Perfectionism

**Lord Jesus,** *I renounce the lie that my sense of worth is dependent upon my ability to perform. I announce the truth that my identity and sense of worth is found in who I am as Your child. I renounce seeking the approval and acceptance of other people, and I choose to believe that I am already approved and accepted in Christ, because of His death and resurrection for me. I choose to believe the truth that I have been saved, not by deeds done in righteousness, but according to Your mercy. I choose to believe that I am no longer under the curse of the law, because Christ became a* *curse for me. I receive the free gift of life in Christ and choose to abide in Him. I renounce striving for perfection by living under the law. By Your grace, Heavenly Father, I choose from this day forward to walk by faith in the power of Your Holy Spirit according to what You have said is true. In Jesus' name I pray.* **Amen.**

### Eating Disorders or Self-Mutilation

**Lord Jesus,** *I renounce the lie that my value as a person is dependent upon my appearance or performance. I renounce cutting or abusing myself, vomiting, using laxatives, or starving myself as a means of being in control, altering my appearance, or trying to cleanse myself of evil. I announce that only the blood of the Lord Jesus Christ cleanses me from sin. I realize I have been bought with a price and my body, the temple of the Holy Spirit, belongs to God. Therefore, I choose to glorify God in my body. I renounce the lie that I am evil or that any part of my body is evil. Thank You that You accept me just the way I am in Christ. In Jesus' name I pray.* **Amen.**

### Substance Abuse

**Lord Jesus,** *I confess that I have misused sub-*stances (alcohol, tobacco, food, prescription or street drugs) *for the purpose of pleasure, to escape reality, or to cope with difficult problems. I confess that I have abused my body and programmed my mind in* *harmful ways. I have quenched the Holy Spirit as well. Thank You for Your forgiveness. I renounce any satanic connection or influence in my life through my misuse of food or chemicals. I cast my anxieties onto Christ who loves me. I commit myself to yield no longer to substance abuse, but instead I choose to allow the Holy Spirit to direct and empower me. In Jesus' name I pray.* **Amen.**

## CONCLUSION

Suppose you have a skeleton in your closet—something that you have done wrong that you have never addressed with God or shared with anybody. What does the liar, the deceiver, the accuser of the brethren do? He knocks at your door and says, "I want to talk with you about the skeleton in your closet." Immediately, you feel anxious, guilty, and condemned, because you know you have a skeleton. If you opened the door, everyone would be able to see it.

Now suppose that you have completely repented of your sin. There is no longer a skeleton in your closet. The Bible tells you that God has totally cleansed and forgiven you

On the basis of Scripture, what you have done in going through the Steps is to reduce those experiences to memories. You are now free from the past and the sin that entangled you.

and that He will never again bring up that sin and use it against you. But Satan continues to knock at the door and tell you that he wants to talk about the skeleton in your closet. This time, however, you don't feel the same anxiety and guilt. You still remember that there used to be a skeleton in the closet, but you know it's not there anymore.

There is a big difference between an unresolved conflict from our past and only the memory of the conflict. On the basis of Scripture, what you have done in going through the Steps is to reduce those experiences to memories. You are now free from the past and the sin that entangled you. It no longer has any hold on you, and God will never use it against you now or in the future.

# Chapter Eight

## Overcoming Ancestral Sins

The last issue that needs to be resolved is related to ancestral sins that are passed on from one generation to another and spiritual attacks that come from the enemy. This step is crucial for those who come from very dysfunctional families or families involved in cults or the occult. This step breaks the final links of bondage that have chained you to your past. You cannot passively take your places in Christ; you must actively choose to accept yourself as a new creation in Christ and take your place in the family of God.

## The Influence of Heritage

Unless we make concerted efforts to do otherwise, we will perpetuate the habits, customs, and traditions passed on in our families for generations. The families we were born into and the way we have been raised shaped our present beliefs and behaviors. Some of those family traits can be very good, and others not so good. Jesus said, "A pupil is not above his teacher; but everyone, after he has been fully trained, will be like his teacher."[148] Our personalities and temperaments have been mostly established by the time we are five years old, and nobody has contributed more to our early development than our parents.

This generational connection is clearly observed in cycles of abuse. The abused become abusers. This cycle is passed on genetically, environmentally and spiritually.

First, we can be genetically predisposed to certain strengths and weaknesses. However, that does not make us alcoholics, or drug addicts, or gay. We took on those traits by the choices we make, but some may be more vulnerable than others due to genetic differences.

Second, the environment we were raised in is the biggest contributor to our development. This process of learning is more caught that taught. The actions of our parents have spoken louder than their words. If you were raised in a home where pornography was left around the house, you will struggle with lust more than the person who was raised in a morally responsible home. Mental strongholds are formed primarily from the environments in which we were raised. By environment, I mean the friends we had, the neighborhoods we played in, the churches we went to (or didn't go to) and the parents (or single parent or guardian) who raised us.

The third contributor to our development is spiritual. In the Ten Commandments, God said, "You shall not make for yourself an idol, or any likeness of what is in heaven above or on the earth beneath or in the water under the earth. You shall not worship them or serve them; for I, the Lord your God, am a jealous God, visiting the iniquity of the fathers on the children, on the third and the fourth generations of those who hate Me, but showing loving kindness to thousands, to those who love Me and keep My commandments."[149] God blesses those who are obedient to His covenant to the thousandth generation but the iniquities of those who are disobedient are passed on to the third and fourth generations.

## GOING THROUGH STEP SEVEN

Ask the Lord to reveal your ancestral sins and then renounce them as follows:

*Dear Heavenly Father, please reveal to my mind all the sins of my ancestors that have been passed down through family lines. Since I am a new creation in Christ, I want to experience my freedom from those influences and walk in my new identity as a child of God. In Jesus' name I pray. **Amen**.*

*Lord, I renounce* (Confess all the family sins that God brings to your mind). ***Amen**.*

Satan and people may curse us, but it will not have any affect on us unless we believe it. We cannot passively take our place in Christ; we must actively and intentionally choose to submit to God and resist the devil. Then he will flee from us. Complete this final step with the following declaration and prayer:

## DECLARATION

*I here and now reject and disown all the sins of my ancestors. As one who has been delivered from the domain of darkness and transferred into the kingdom of God's Son, I declare myself to be free from those harmful influences. I am no longer "in Adam." I am now alive "in Christ." Therefore I am the recipient of the blessings of God upon my life as I choose to love and obey Him. As one who has been crucified and raised with Christ and who sits with Him in heavenly places, I renounce any and all satanic attacks and assignments directed against me and my ministry. Every curse placed on me was broken when Christ became a curse for me by dying on the cross* (Galatians 3:13). *I reject any and every way in which Satan may claim ownership of me. I belong to the Lord Jesus Christ who purchased me with His own precious blood. I declare myself to be fully and eternally signed over and committed to the Lord Jesus Christ. Therefore, having submitted to God and by His authority, I now resist the devil, and I command every spiritual enemy of the Lord Jesus Christ to leave my presence. I put on the armor of God, and I stand against Satan's temptations, accusations, and deceptions. From this day forward I will seek to do only the will of my Heavenly Father.*

## PRAYER

*Dear Heavenly Father, I come to You as Your child, bought out of slavery to sin by the blood of the Lord Jesus Christ. You are the Lord of the universe and the Lord of my Life. I submit my body to You as a living and holy sacrifice. May You be glorified through my life and body. I now ask You to fill me with Your Holy Spirit. I commit myself to the renewing of my mind in order that I may prove that Your will is good, acceptable, and perfect for me. I desire nothing more than to be like You. I pray, believe, and do all this in the wonderful name of Jesus, my Lord and Savior. Amen.*

## MAINTAINING YOUR FREEDOM

Experiencing your freedom in Christ is exciting, but what you have gained must be maintained. You have won an important battle, but the war goes on. To maintain your freedom in Christ and grow in the grace of God, you must continue renewing your mind to the truth of God's word. If you become aware of lies you have believed, renounce them and choose the truth. If more painful memories surface, then forgive those who hurt you and renounce any sinful part you played. Many people choose to go through the Steps to Freedom in Christ again to make sure they have dealt with all their issues. Some times new issues will surface. Some go through the Steps again as a periodic "house cleaning."

After going though the Steps, people sometimes have thoughts like: *Nothing has really changed. You're the same person you always were. It didn't work.* In most cases you should just ignore those thoughts. We are not called to dispel the darkness; we are called to turn on the light. You don't get rid of negative thoughts by rebuking every one; you get rid of them by repenting and choosing the truth.

I encourage you to read *Victory Over the Darkness* (Regal Books, 2000) and *The Bondage Breaker* (Harvest House, 2000). To continue growing in the grace of God:

1. Get rid of or destroy any cult or occult objects in your home. (See Acts 19:18-20.)
2. Get involved in a small group ministry where you can be a real person, and be part of a church where God's truth is taught with kindness and grace.

3. Read and meditate on the truth of God's Word each day.

4. Don't let your mind be passive, especially concerning what you watch and listen to (music, TV, etc.). Take every thought captive to the obedience of Christ.

5. Be open and honest with God in prayer. (See *Praying By the Power of the Spirit*, Harvest House, 2003).

## DAILY PRAYER AND DECLARATION

*Dear Heavenly Father, I praise You and honor You as my Lord and Savior. You are in control of all things. I thank You that You are always with me and will never leave me nor forsake me. You are the only all-powerful and only wise God. You are kind and loving in all Your ways. I love You and thank You that I am united with Christ and spiritually alive in Him. I choose not to love the world or the things in the world, and I crucify the flesh and all its passions.*

*Thank You for the life I now have in Christ. I ask You to fill me with the Holy Spirit so I can be guided by You and not carry out the desires of the flesh. I declare my total dependence upon You, and I take my stand against Satan and all his lying ways. I choose to believe the truth of God's Word despite what my feelings may say. I refuse to be discouraged; You are the God of all hope. Nothing is too difficult for You. I am confident that You will supply all my needs as I seek to live according to Your Word. I thank You that I can be content and live a responsible life through Christ who strengthens me.*

*I now take my stand against Satan and command him and all his evil spirits to depart from me. I choose to put on the full armor of God so I may be able to stand firm against all the devil's schemes. I submit my body as a living and holy sacrifice to You, and I choose to renew my mind by Your living Word. By so doing I will be able to prove that Your will is good, acceptable, and perfect for me. In the name of my Lord and Savior, Jesus Christ, I pray.* **Amen.**

## BEDTIME PRAYER

***Thank You, Lord,*** *that You have brought me into Your family and have blessed me with every spiritual blessing in the heavenly places in Christ Jesus. Thank You for this time of renewal and refreshment through sleep. I accept it as one of Your blessings for Your children and I trust You to guard my mind and my body during my sleep.*

*As I have thought about You and Your truth during the day, I choose to let those good thoughts continue in my mind while I am asleep. I commit myself to You for Your protection against every attempt of Satan and his demons to attack me during sleep. Guard my mind from nightmares. I renounce all fear and cast every anxiety upon You, Lord. I commit myself to You as my rock, my fortress, and my strong tower. May Your peace be upon this place of rest. In the strong name of the Lord Jesus Christ I pray.* **Amen.**

## PRAYER FOR SPIRITUAL CLEANSING
### *Home/Apartment/Room*

After removing and destroying all objects of false worship, pray this prayer aloud in every room:

**Heavenly Father,** *I acknowledge that You are the Lord of heaven and earth. In Your sovereign power and love, You have entrusted me with many things. Thank You for this place to live. I claim my home as a place of spiritual safety for me and my family and ask for Your protection from all the attacks of the enemy. As a child of God, raised up and seated with Christ in the heavenly places, I command every evil spirit claiming ground in this place, based on the activities of past or present occupants, including me and my family, to leave and never return. I renounce all demonic assignments directed against this place. I ask You, Heavenly Father, to post Your holy angels around this place to guard it from any and all* *attempts of the enemy to enter and disturb Your purposes for me and my family. I thank You, Lord, for doing this in the name of the Lord Jesus Christ.* **Amen.**

## PRAYER FOR LIVING IN A NON-CHRISTIAN ENVIRONMENT

After removing and destroying all objects of false worship from your possession, pray this aloud in the place where you live:

> **Thank You,** *Heavenly Father, for a place to live and to be renewed by sleep. I ask You to set aside my room* (or portion of this room) *as a place of spiritual safety for me. I renounce any allegiance given to false gods or spirits by other occupants. I renounce any claim to this room* (space) *by Satan based on the activities of past or present occupants, including me. On the basis of my position as a child of God and joint-heir with Christ, who has all authority in heaven and on earth, I command all evil spirits to leave this place and never return. I ask You, Heavenly Father, to station Your holy angels to protect me while I live here. In Jesus' mighty name I pray.* **Amen.**

Paul prays in Ephesians 1:18, "I pray the eyes of your heart may be enlightened, so that you will know what is the hope of His calling, what are the riches of the glory of His inheritance in the saints, and what is the surpassing greatness of His power toward us who believe." Jesus has met your needs for acceptance, security, and significance. Read the following list aloud, morning and evening, for the next few weeks. Think about what you are reading and let the truth of who you are in Christ renew your mind. This is your inheritance in Christ.

# IN CHRIST

I renounce the lie that I am rejected, unloved, or shameful. ***In Christ I am accepted.***

*God says:*

I am God's child. (John 1:12)

I am Christ's friend. (John 15:5)

I have been justified. (Romans 5:1)

I am united with the Lord and I am one spirit with Him. (1 Corinthians 6:17)

I have been bought with a price: I belong to God. (1 Corinthians 6:19, 20)

I am a member of Christ's body. (1 Corinthians 12:27)

I am a saint, a holy one. (Ephesians 1:1)

I have been adopted as God's child. (Ephesians 1:5)

I have direct access to God through the Holy Spirit. (Ephesians 2:18)

I have been redeemed and forgiven of all my sins. (Colossians 1:14)

I am complete in Christ. (Colossians 2:10)

I renounce the lie that I am guilty, unprotected, alone, or abandoned. *In Christ I am secure.*

*God says:*

> I am free from condemnation. (Romans 8:1, 2)
>
> I am assured that all things work together for good. (Romans 8:28)
>
> I am free from any condemning charges against me. (Romans 8:31-34)
>
> I cannot be separated from the love of God. (Romans 8:35-39)
>
> I have been established, anointed, and sealed by God. (2 Corinthians 1:21, 22)
>
> I am confident that the good work God has begun in me will be perfected. (Philippians 1:6)
>
> I am a citizen of heaven. (Philippians 3:20)
>
> I am hidden with Christ in God. (Colossians 3:3)
>
> I have not been given a spirit of fear, but of power, love, and discipline. (2 Timothy 1:7)
>
> I can find grace and mercy to help in time of need. (Hebrews 4:16)
>
> I am born of God and the evil one cannot touch me. (1 John 5:18)

I renounce the lie that I am worthless, inadequate, helpless, or hopeless. *In Christ I am significant.*

*God says:*

> I am the salt of the earth and the light of the world. (Matthew 5:13, 14)

I am a branch of the true vine, Jesus, a channel of His life. (John 15:1,5)

I have been chosen and appointed by God to bear fruit. (John 15:16)

I am a personal, Spirit-empowered witness of Christ's. (Acts 1:8)

I am a temple of God. (1 Corinthians 3:16)

I am a minister of reconciliation for God. (2 Corinthians 5:17-21)

I am God's coworker. (2 Corinthians 6:1)

I am seated with Christ in the heavenly realm. (Ephesians 2:6)

I am God's workmanship, created for good works. (Ephesians 2:10)

I may approach God with freedom and confidence. (Ephesians 3:12)

I can do all things through Christ who strengthens me! (Philippians 4:13)

*I am not the great "I Am,"*
*but by the grace of God I am what I am.*

(See Exodus 3:14; John 8:24, 28, 58; 1 Corinthians 15:10.)

# ABOUT THE AUTHOR

**Dr. Neil T. Anderson** is Founder and President Emeritus of Freedom in Christ Ministries. He has over 35 years of pastoral and teaching experience and was formerly chairman of the Practical Theology Department at Talbot School of Theology. Neil has authored or co-authored over 50 books on Christ-centered living, including the best-selling *Victory Over the Darkness, The Bondage Breaker, Discipleship Counseling* and *The Daily Discipler*. He and his wife, Joanne, currently reside in Franklin, Tennessee.

# Core Message and Materials

*Victory Over the Darkness* with study guide, audiobook and DVD
(Regal Books, 2000). With over 1,000,000 copies in print, this core
book explains who you are in Christ, how to walk by faith in the
power of the Holy Spirit, how to be transformed by the renewing of
your mind, how to experience emotional freedom, and how to relate
to one another in Christ.

*The Bondage Breaker* with study guide, audiobook
(Harvest House Publishers, 2000) and DVD (Regal Books, 2006).
With over 1,000,000 copies in print, this book explains spiritual warfare, what our protection is, ways that we are vulnerable, and how
we can live a liberated life in Christ.

*Breaking Through to Spiritual Maturity* (Regal Books, 2000).
This curriculum teaches the basic message of Discipleship
Counseling Ministries.

*Discipleship Counseling* with DVD (Regal Books, 2003).
This book combines the concepts of discipleship and counseling and
teaches the practical integration of theology and psychology for
helping Christians resolve their personal and spiritual conflicts
through repentance and faith in God.

*Steps to Freedom in Christ* and interactive videocassette
(Regal Books, 2004). This discipleship counseling tool helps
Christians resolve their personal and spiritual conflicts.

*Beta: The Next Step in Your Journey with Christ*
(Regal Books, 2004) is a discipleship course for Sunday School class-
es and small groups. The kit includes a teacher's guide, a student
guide and two DVDs covering 12 lessons and the Steps to Freedom
in Christ. This course is designed to enable new and stagnant
believers to resolve personal and spiritual conflicts and be established alive and free in Christ.

*The Daily Discipler* (Regal Books, 2005). This practical systematic
theology is a culmination of all of Neil's books covering the major
doctrines of the Christian faith and the problems Christians face.
It is a five-day-per-week, one-year study that will thoroughly ground
believers in their faith.

## Victory Over the Darkness Series:

*Overcoming a Negative Self-Image*, with Dave Park
(Regal Books, 2003)

*Overcoming Addictive Behavior*, with Mike Quarles
(Regal Books, 2003)

*Overcoming Doubt*
(Regal Books, 2004)

*Overcoming Depression*, with Joanne Anderson
(Regal Books, 2004)

## Bondage Breaker Series:

*Praying by the Power of the Spirit*
(Harvest House Publishers, 2003)

*Finding God's Will in Spiritually Deceptive Times*
(Harvest House Publishers, 2003)

*Finding Freedom in a Sex-Obsessed World*
(Harvest House Publishers, 2004)

## Specialized Books:

*God's Power at Work in You*, with Dr. Robert Saucy
(Harvest House Publishers, 2001). A thorough analysis of sanctification and practical instruction on how we grow in Christ.

*Released from Bondage*, with Judith King and Dr. Fernando
Garzon (Thomas Nelson, 2002). This book has personal accounts of
how defeated Christians resolved their conflicts and found their
freedom in Christ with explanatory notes by Dr. Anderson, and how
the message of Discipleship Counseling can be applied to therapy
with research results.

*Daily in Christ*, with Joanne Anderson
(Harvest House Publishers, 2000). This popular daily devotional is
also being used by thousands of Internet subscribers every day.

*Who I Am in Christ* (Regal Books, 2001). In 36 short chapters,
this book describes who you are in Christ and how He meets your
deepest needs.

*Freedom from Addiction*, with Mike and Julia Quarles
(Regal Books, 1997). Using Mike's testimony, this book explains the
nature of chemical addictions and how to overcome them in Christ.

*One Day at a Time*, with Mike and Julia Quarles
(Regal Books, 2000). This devotional helps those who struggle with
addictive behaviors and explains how to discover the grace of God on
a daily basis.

*Freedom from Fear*, with Rich Miller (Harvest House Publishers,
1999). This book explains anxiety disorders and how to overcome
them.

*Extreme Church Makeover*, with Charles Mylander
(Regal Books, 2006). This book offers guidelines and encouragement
for resolving seemingly impossible corporate conflicts in the church
and also provides leaders with a primary means for church
growth—releasing the power of God in the church.

*Experiencing Christ Together,* with Dr. Charles Mylander
(Regal Books, 2006.) This book explains God's divine plan for marriage and the steps that couples can take to resolve their difficulties.

*Christ Centered Therapy*, with Dr. Terry and Julie Zuehlke
(Zondervan Publishing House, 2000). A textbook explaining the
practical integration of theology and psychology for professional
counselors.

*Getting Anger Under Control*, with Rich Miller (Harvest House
Publishers, 1999). This book explains the basis for anger and how to
control it.

*The Biblical Guide to Alternative Medicine*, with Dr. Michael
Jacobson (Regal Books, 2003). This book develops a grid by which
you can evaluate medical practices, and then applies the grid to the
world's most recognized philosophies of medicine and health.

*Breaking the Strongholds of Legalism*, with Rich Miller and
Paul Travis (Harvest House Publishers, 2003). An explanation of
legalism and how to overcome it.

# To purchase these resources contact:

---

**e3 Resources**
317 Main Street
Suite 207
Franklin, Tennessee 37064
(888) 354-9411
info@e3resources.org

---

**Freedom In Christ Ministries**
9051 Executive Park Drive
Ste. 503
Knoxville, Tennessee 37923
(865) 342-4000
info@ficm.org

# Notes

## INTRODUCTION

1. Mark 1:15
2. 2 Corinthians 5:17
3. Colossians 1:13
4. Ephesians 2:10

## CHAPTER ONE: REDEMPTION HISTORY

5. Genesis 1:1
6. Genesis 1:26
7. Ephesians 2:1
8. Romans 8:22
9. Genesis 3:14, 15
10. Galatians 3:24
11. John 8:42; 14:10; 17:7
12. Romans 3:23
13. Hebrews 9:22
14. 2 Corinthians 5:21
15. John 10:10
16. John 6:48

17. John 14:6
18. Acts 4:12
19. John 8:32
20. John 11:25, 26
21. Ephesians 2:8, 9
22. John 1:12
23. 1 John 3:1
24. Matthew 6:9
25. Romans 8:16
26. Philippians 4:19
27. 1 Corinthians 15:1-8
28. John 14:17
29. 1 John 3:8
30. John 16:11
31. John 12:31
32. 1 John 5:19
33. Revelation 12:9
34. Colossians 2:15
35. John 8:44
36. Ephesians 2:4-6
37. Matthew 28:18
38. Matthew 28:19, 20
39. Ephesians 6:10
40. Acts 26:20
41. Acts 2:38, 39
42. Philippians 4:7
43. Romans 10:9, 10

# CHAPTER TWO: OVERCOMING FALSE GUIDANCE

44. Proverbs 28:13
45. Matthew 3:7, 8
46. Romans 12:2
47. 1 Timothy 4:1
48. Matthew 24:24
49. 2 Corinthians 11:13-15

50. Matthew 26:63; John 8:58; 1 Corinthians 3:11; Revelation 19:16
51. 2 Corinthians 4:4; 11:3, 4, 14
52. James 4:7
53. Ephesians 1:20, 21; Colossians 2:15; 1 Peter 3:22
54. Acts 19:11-16
55. 1 Corinthians 6:19; Philippians 4:19

## CHAPTER THREE: OVERCOMING DECEPTION

56. John 8:31, 32 (NKJV)
57. Ephesians 6:14
58. Psalm 51:6
59. Psalm 32:2
60. 1 John 1:6, 7
61. John 8:44
62. 2 Corinthians 4:4; Revelation 12:9
63. 2 Corinthians 10:4, 5
64. 1 Timothy 4:1

## CHAPTER FOUR: OVERCOMING THE BONDAGE OF BITTERNESS

65. Romans 12:19
66. Proverbs 14:10
67. Colossians 2:18
68. 2 Corinthians. 10:5
69. Hebrews 12:15
70. Job 42:6
71. 2 Corinthians 5:21
72. Matthew 26:38
73. Luke 23:34
74. Romans 6:10
75. Ephesians 4:31, 32
76. 2 Corinthians 2:10, 11
77. Ephesians 4:26, 27, 31, 32

78. Romans 6:23
79. Titus 3:4, 5
80. Ephesians 2:8
81. Luke 6:36
82. 2 Peter 1:4
83. 1 John 4:8
84. John 13:35
85. Romans 8:1
86. Hebrews 12:15
87. Romans 12:18

## CHAPTER FIVE: OVERCOMING REBELLION

88. Matthew 6:24
89. Genesis 3:5
90. Galatians 5:23
91. 1 Samuel 15:23
92. Romans 13:1, 2
93. Acts 5:29
94. Daniel 1:9
95. Matthew 6:9-13
96. Hebrews 13:17
97. See Numbers 14:11-19
98. 1 Timothy 2:1, 2
99. 1 Peter 2:18-20
100. Matthew 6:11
101. Matthew 6:12
102. Acts 8:23
103. Matthew 6:13
104. 1 Peter 2:14
105. Daniel 6:7
106. James 1:27
107. Ephesians 5:21
108. Ephesians 5:21-24; 1 Peter 3:1-6
109. Ephesians 5:25-33; 1 Peter 3:7
110. Colossians 3:11

111. Galatians 3:28
112. Matthew 20:25-27
113. 1 Peter 2:1
114. 1 Peter 2: 2-17 (NKJV)
115. 1 Peter 2:9, 10
116. 1 Peter 3:8-12
117. James 4:7

## CHAPTER SIX: OVERCOMING PRIDE

118. Isaiah 14:13-15
119. Mark 6:48
120. 2 Chronicles 26:3
121. 1 Corinthians 10:12 (NKJV)
122. Colossians 2:18
123. Romans 12:3
124. 1 Corinthians 15:10
125. Philippians 3:3
126. John 15:8
127. Matthew 5:16
128. See John 15:5
129. Ephesians 3:12
130. 2 Peter 2:10
131. 1 John 2:16
132. Luke 22:31, 32
133. See Ephesians 1:3-14
134. Ephesians 1:18
135. James 4:6

## CHAPTER SEVEN: OVERCOMING HABITUAL SIN

136. Galatians 5:17
137. 2 Corinthians 10:5
138. James 1:14, 15
139. See 1 John 1:5-9
140. See James 4:7

141. 1 Thessalonians 5:22

142. Romans 12:2

143. See Galatians 5:16

144. See Romans 6:12, 13; 13:14; 2 Corinthians 4:2;
     James 4:1; 1 Peter 2:11; 5:8

145. See Romans 8:1, 2

146. Romans 6: 13

147. See Romans 12:1

# CHAPTER EIGHT: OVERCOMING ANCESTRAL SINS

148. Luke 6:40

149. Exodus 20:4-6

Printed in the United States
99462LV00002B/64-66/A